Risk
Management

Andrew Holmes

FINANCE

05.10

Fast track route to managing risk

Covers the key areas of risk management, from understanding the nature of risk and how it manifests itself in organizations to managing the risks of electronic commerce and the risks imposed by globalisation

Examples and lessons from some of the world's most successful businesses, including Shell, Xerox and Nike, and ideas from the smartest thinkers, including Peter Schwartz, Blair Gibb, Peter Bernstein, Kees Van Der Heijden and Jean Camp

Includes a glossary of key concepts and a comprehensive resources guide

>EXPRESS EXEC.COM<

essential management thinking at your fingertips

Copyright © Capstone Publishing 2002

The right of Andrew Holmes to be identified as the author of this work has been asserted in accordance with the Copyright, Designs and Patents Act 1988

First published 2002 by
Capstone Publishing (a Wiley company)
8 Newtec Place
Magdalen Road
Oxford OX4 1RE
United Kingdom
http://www.capstoneideas.com

CIP catalogue records for this book are available from the British Library and the US Library of Congress

ISBN 1-84112-341-2

This book is printed on acid-free paper

Substantial discounts on bulk quantities of Capstone books are available to corporations, professional associations and other organizations. Please contact Capstone for more details on +44 (0)1865 798 623 or (fax) +44 (0)1865 240 941 or (e-mail) info@wiley-capstone.co.uk

FSC
Mixed Sources
Product group from well-managed
forests and other controlled sources
Cert no. SGS-COC-2953
www.fsc.org
© 1996 Forest Stewardship Council

Contents

Introduction to ExpressExec   v

05.10.01 Introduction to Risk Management   1
05.10.02 What is Risk Management?   5
05.10.03 The Evolution of Risk Management   15
05.10.04 The E-Dimension   27
05.10.05 The Global Dimension   37
05.10.06 The State of the Art   45
05.10.07 In Practice: Risk Management Success Stories   61
05.10.08 Key Concepts and Thinkers   75
05.10.09 Resources   95
05.10.10 Ten Steps to Making Risk Management Work   109

Frequently Asked Questions (FAQs)   117
Index   119

Introduction to ExpressExec

ExpressExec is 3 million words of the latest management thinking compiled into 10 modules. Each module contains 10 individual titles forming a comprehensive resource of current business practice written by leading practitioners in their field. From brand management to balanced scorecard, ExpressExec enables you to grasp the key concepts behind each subject and implement the theory immediately. Each of the 100 titles is available in print and electronic formats.

Through the ExpressExec.com Website you will discover that you can access the complete resource in a number of ways:

» printed books or e-books;
» e-content – PDF or XML (for licensed syndication) adding value to an intranet or Internet site;
» a corporate e-learning/knowledge management solution providing a cost-effective platform for developing skills and sharing knowledge within an organization;
» bespoke delivery – tailored solutions to solve your need.

Why not visit www.expressexec.com and register for free key management briefings, a monthly newsletter and interactive skills checklists. Share your ideas about ExpressExec and your thoughts about business today.

Please contact elound@wiley-capstone.co.uk for more information.

Introduction to Risk Management

Why is risk management important? Chapter 1 considers the importance of risk and covers:

» the difference between personal risk and corporate risk; and
» the broad nature of risks that organizations now have to face.

"The revolutionary idea that defines the boundary between modern times and the past is the mastery of risk . . . "

Peter Bernstein, economics and risk guru

"There is nothing wrong with risk. It is the lifeblood of business and the test of entrepreneurs and managers. What matters is how you handle risk and the culture in which you operate."

John Holliwell, managing director of Smith Williamson Consultancy

We live in uncertain times. Competitive markets, globalization, booms, busts, recessions, technological change, war, climatic change, and so on. All present risks to a varying degree.

In many respects we are all used to dealing with a certain level of risk within our daily lives. After all, walking across the road has an inherent risk associated with it. But unless we are doing something that departs significantly from our daily routine, such as jumping out of a plane for example, we tend to take risk for granted and we often don't give it a second thought. Also, at the individual level, if we take a risk and fail to manage it properly, the damage is limited to us, and maybe our near relatives.

The management of risk for organizations is not as simple, for two reasons. First, because the implications of poor risk management can have significant impacts for a wider number of stakeholders including shareholders, employees, the national and local economies. And second, because the nature of risk within organizations is far more complex than the simple risks we have to manage as individuals. Managing risk is an essential skill of all modern corporations. And, for those who manage risk well, the rewards can be great. For example Tesco, the UK food retailer, has consistently led the competition by being the first to market with new innovations such as loyalty cards and Internet grocery shopping. Being first to market offers great first mover opportunity, but it also involves the careful management of risk. Tesco's foray into the Internet shopping arena was not without its problems, as early on, the technology was not as robust as it needed to be (see Chapter 4 for the general risks imposed by the Internet). However, through ongoing improvements, Tesco's Internet shopping offering has gone from strength to strength and has captured the market. It is clear from this example that if there were no risks, there would be no opportunity to make a profit or succeed where others fail.

Successful organizations therefore tend to be excellent risk managers, not only because they understand the risks they face, but also because of how they manage them. Conversely, those organizations that are poor at risk management spend no time scanning the risk horizon, instead leaving their futures to fate. This invariably means shocks, falling market share, take-overs and missed opportunities. Unfortunately, managing risk is no longer a simple process. Drivers such as technological change and globalization have increased the systemic nature of risk. They are no longer isolated events but interconnected and liable to cause a chain reaction that can ripple around the world. For example, during the late 1990s we witnessed the effects of Russia defaulting on its domestic loans and the impact of the failure of the Long-Term Capital Management hedge fund. In both cases, the impacts were felt across the global financial system and required central government intervention either by propping up the affected currencies or by dropping interest rates to calm the markets.

The computerization of the workplace and the levels of IT dependency that now exist means the risks associated with the failure of IT systems owe one of the most potent sources of operational risk within any organization. Globalization, too, has added new risks, especially those associated with pollution, the environment, and the exploitation of workforces. Multinational companies now have to concern themselves with the negative effects of their actions across the globe and the associated impact on their share price and market share. We saw what happens when corporate actions are poorly judged when Shell tried to dispose of the Brent Spar North Sea oil storage tank in 1995.

Ultimately, all risks have a financial impact. And, because of this, managing risk is no longer restricted to financial institutions or the financial director. Within the modern corporation, risk management must encapsulate managing strategic, business, operational, and technical risks, rather than those associated with pure finance such as credit, interest rate, and currency risk.

This resource takes a very broad scan across the risk management horizon and will provide the reader with a foundation of what risk management means for today's organization. It discusses what risk management is (Chapter 2), the emergence of risk management as a discipline (Chapter 3), the new risks posed by the electronic channel (Chapter 4) and those risks that have arise from globalization (Chapter 5). Chapter 6 discusses some of the latest approaches to managing risk, and Chapter 7 outlines some of the approaches used by organizations to manage them. Chapter 8 gives a glossary of common risk management terms and concepts. Useful sources of information on risk and risk management are highlighted in Chapter 9, and Chapter 10 provides 10 steps to success.

What is Risk Management?

Most organizations manage their risks badly and don't understand the importance or benefits of good risk management. Chapter 2 therefore covers some of the basics, including:

» categories of risk;
» levels of risk sophistication;
» approaches to managing risk – as a general process and within banking;
» the consequences of poor risk management; and
» the advantages of risk management.

"Risk means being exposed to the possibility of a bad outcome ... Risk management means taking deliberate action to shift the odds in your favour – increasing the odds of good outcomes and reducing the odds of bad outcomes."

Dan Borge, managing director and partner, Bankers Trust

"Traditional risk management in a corporation tends to gravitate toward thinking about that which can be insured against. It focuses on risks that insurance companies either cover or explicitly refuse to cover and on the proper financial management of those costs and benefits."

Peter Schwartz, scenario planning expert and author
and Blair Gibb, international trade specialist

Risk management is about following a deliberate set of actions designed to identify, quantify, manage, and then monitor those things, events or actions that could lead to financial loss. This implies that risk management is an active process requiring commitment and focus. But in many instances, there is insufficient data about a risk to define it precisely. As a result, risk management involves a large degree of judgment and requires the organization to make certain assumptions about the future. For example, whereas assessing the likelihood of a road accident is quite easy, assessing the risk of nuclear meltdown is very difficult. This is because in the case of road accidents, there is plenty of information available against which the risk can be assessed, but in the nuclear meltdown case there is very little. This separates risk (which can be managed) from uncertainty (which generally cannot be managed without the construction of theoretical models). Therefore, in order to manage risks effectively, it is necessary to categorize the types of risk that organizations are exposed to and then manage them accordingly.

CATEGORIES OF RISK

Risk falls into five broad categories:

» *Strategic risk.* This is associated with those risks that can affect the strategic direction and survival of the organization. Factors that play into this category include the macroeconomic risks created by the fiscal policies of central and federal governments, as well as the impacts of disruptive technologies, such as the Internet. Such risks are also associated with poor business decisions and direction setting, and extend to such things as mergers and acquisitions. It is well known, for example, that mergers and acquisitions are notorious for failing, with up to 80% never realizing the benefits expected of them. Considering the amount of money invested in such ventures, the very fact that so many fail suggests poor risk management.

» *Business/financial risk*. This covers those risks that can affect the business in terms of its general financial viability. It includes risks associated with the market in which the organization operates (market risk), as well as the ability to finance growth through loans (credit risk). These risks are generally well understood, with a large number of financial instruments, and techniques available to the risk manager.

» *Program and project risk*. This is the risk that a major change initiative could fail or the benefits expected of it might not materialize. With an increasing use of projects and programs to drive through change within organizations, this type of risk is often closely associated with strategic risk, as failure can have significant impacts on the organization. Moreover, with the increasing complexity of organizations, managing this type of risk is fast becoming an essential skill.

» *Operational risk*. This is a wide-ranging category of risk that includes the failure of any aspect of a business's operations. This includes management failure, system and software failure, human error, process inefficiencies, and procedural failures. Although comparatively new, it is recognized as being an important part of an overall risk management framework.

» *Technological risk*. This is different from operational risk in that it is associated with bringing new technology products to market and introducing new technology (and IT systems) into the organizational setting, both of which are high risk ventures.

LEVELS OF SOPHISTICATION

According to Chris Frost, David Allen, James Porter, and Philip Bloodworth, authors of *Operational Risk and Resilience*, an organization's appetite for risk sits along a continuum that ranges from taking a reactive stance to one that is fully integrated with all organizational activities and linked to the achievement of increased shareholder value. This continuum has five levels.

1 The lowest level of sophistication is the reactive stance. Here, risks are only ever dealt with when they turn into live issues (when they materialize) or when crisis strikes. Such organizations lurch from one problem to another without ever taking the trouble to pre-sensitize themselves to the risks they face.

2 A slightly more sophisticated approach is where the organization understands the importance of risk management and takes the trouble to identify and manage them more actively. Such organizations tend to seek out best practice and view risk in a much wider context (and not just financially).

3 Those organizations that understand the relationship between risk and change recognize the need to manage risks throughout the organization and usually have some form of risk management framework in place to ensure consistency of approach.

4 High maturity organizations fully understand the link between risk and reward. They recognize that with every risk there is an associated opportunity that can be exploited. These organizations are often market leaders and are willing to take risks to achieve their strategic objectives.

5 The ultimate in risk sophistication is where organizations integrate risk management with the goal of enhancing shareholder value. As a result they shift the responsibility for risk management away from the traditional areas of audit and compliance to everyone within the organization.

APPROACHES TO MANAGING RISK

The basic form of risk management involves four continuous stages.

» *Identification*. This involves the organization identifying the types of risk it might be exposed to. Some are more obvious and manageable than others. The key point is to identify those risks that can be managed. Identifying risks that are way outside of your control means that little can be done to manage them, resulting in time and effort being spent to no avail. In such instances, it would be better to develop contingency and business continuity plans to address the risk once it has materialized.

» *Quantification*. This involves assessing the severity of the risk which in its simplest form is the product of its impact (which is usually assessed in terms of financial loss) and probability or likelihood of occurrence. Because it can be very difficult to make precise assessments of probability and impact, most organizations rate each dimension using high, medium, and low, where each represents a range rather than a precise figure. This makes it easier to rank the risks when it comes to choosing those it intends to manage.

» *Managing or responding*. This requires the organization to establish a course of action that will address the risk. Organizations have five responses. They can *transfer* the risk by passing it to a third party. For example, one of the reasons why so many organizations have outsourced their information technology is to pass the technological risk to those who are better positioned to manage it. They can *avoid* the risk by taking a different course of action. They can *reduce* the risk by taking action that minimizes its impact or probability. They can put some *contingency* in place that allows the organization to cope with the implications of the risk should it materialize. This was an essential component in preparing for Year 2000, for example. Finally, they can *accept* the risk and its consequences. Ultimately, before this strategy is adopted, it is important to understand the impacts of the risk and how much it would cost the organization in terms of money and resources to manage it. Balancing the two will allow an appropriate decision to be made.

» *Monitoring and controlling*. Risks are time-based events and as such their impact and probability will vary with time. This is well known within banking, but less so in the other areas of risk, such as strategic and operational risk. Monitoring risk has two strands to it. The first is to ensure the actions agreed during the response stage are undertaken and their impact on the risk's impact and probability is tracked. And the second is to monitor the risk over time, as other events will cause the risk's probability and impact to increase or decrease.

The four stages above should form part of a documented risk management process with formal risk registers and action plans.

Risk management in banking is different. According to Joël Bessis, risk management within the banking community is principally based upon quantitative measures of risk. He cites three quantitative indicators that are commonly used.

» Sensitivity – this captures the deviation of earnings from such things as interest margins or changes in the mark-to-market values of financial instruments (such as derivatives) with a single unit change in a market parameter such as interest rates, exchange rates, or stock prices.

» Volatility – this captures the variations around the average of a random parameter or target value both positively (upside) and negatively (downside). It is a common measure of the dispersion around the average of a random variable. Volatility is the standard deviation of the values of this variable.

» Downside measures of risk such as value at risk that concentrate on the negative variations only. To allow the effective management of risk, these are usually classed as worst case values. These tend to be the most comprehensive measure of risk because they incorporate both sensitivity and volatility.

Financial institutions manage their risks in a variety of different ways. Market risk (the loss arising from adverse changes in market rates and prices) is often dealt with through the use of hedging transactions such as derivatives. Credit risk (the risk that a customer will default on their loan) is usually managed by setting limits on the amount lent, having credit officers and credit committees to agree to lend money, and varying the interest rate and amount of collateral to match the risk rating of the client.

THE CONSEQUENCES OF POOR RISK MANAGEMENT

It is clear that failing to manage risk can result in financial loss of one kind or another. For example, the failure of governments to manage their economies can lead to boom and bust, recessions and, in extreme cases, depressions. The depression that followed the Wall Street Crash in 1929 was in part caused by the actions of the central banks that raised interest rates in the hope of keeping money and gold from flowing out of their countries. This resulted in the economic problems lasting much longer than was necessary. Similar errors of judgment in the UK during the 1970s led to the International Monetary Fund bailing out the then Labour administration. And more recently, in 1998, we saw the Russian government default on their domestic debt and trigger panic in the emerging markets.

At the strategic level, organizations can be seduced into rushing into investing in speculative bubbles and seeking first mover advantage without thinking about the downside risks. The rush into Internet banking, for example, resulted in many financial institutions investing many millions in the hope of capturing market share. Only when they realized that there were too many banks chasing too few customers was the plug pulled. The same can be said of the technological bubble that burst with the failure of the Internet start-up businesses. This resulted in billions of market capitalization being wiped off the value of telecom and technology stocks overnight (see case below).

WHEN THE DOWNSIDE RISKS ARE TOO GREAT[1]

In a little under a year, JDS Uniphase, the world's largest optical components manufacturer, went from rapid growth, in order to meet a massive upturn in demand, to announcing the biggest loss in corporate history ($56.6bn). The turnaround in fortunes has much to do with the excesses of tech bubble that burst in 2000. But is also associated with the management of risk. Write downs of $44.8bn in relation to the acquisition of various companies over the previous two years were, according to some commentators, a "massive mistake" and a "huge waste of shareholder funds." Although the acquisitions were paid by JDS Uniphase shares and hence the loss was only on paper, they missed the opportunity to use them to purchase non-telecom companies that would have allowed them to weather the storm. In this case the risk management processes did not match the company's risk appetite.

At the project and program level, many hundreds of millions of dollars can be wasted on major change projects and technology programs without any benefit to the organization. For example, the Confirm travel reservation project that failed during the early 1990s cost its backers $125mn and in 1992 the failure of Westpac's CS90 project cost them A$125mn. With an increasing emphasis on projects and programs to deliver strategic change, the impact of poor risk management can be disastrous.

ADVANTAGES OF RISK MANAGEMENT

Actively managing risks has many advantages, including:

» gaining a much better understanding of the risks that are facing the organization and its activities;
» understanding how risks interact;
» identifying the uncertainties that have to be managed, monitored, and controlled at all levels;
» providing input into investment decisions;
» understanding the implications of taking different courses of action;
» assessing the financial implications of investments, lending decisions, and the markets;
» viewing risks as opportunities, rather than threats; and
» providing visibility of the risks that the organization wishes to take deliberately as well as those it needs to guard against and actively avoid.

THE ADVANTAGES OF EFFECTIVE RISK MANAGEMENT

In August 2001 BP's second quarter profits came in at a record $7.9bn, up 25% on the previous year. Yet 10 years ago, BP was almost bankrupt. The achievements of the current chief executive, Lord Browne, who has transformed the company, cannot be overstated. He transformed BP by slashing costs, attacking overcapacity and taking risks by acquiring Amoco and Atlantic Richfield. These acquisitions were made at a time when oil prices were hovering around $10 per barrel and the oil industry was in a poor state of repair. Hindsight suggests he purchased the two rivals at a knock down price, but what it points to is an astute management of risk.

KEY LEARNING POINTS
What is risk management?

1 Risk management is the process of managing the negative consequences of an event.

2 Risk falls into five categories:
   » strategic
   » business/financial
   » program and project
   » technical
   » operational.
3 An organization's appetite for risk defines its approach to risk management.
4 The severity of a risk is defined by the product of its impact and probability.
5 The process of risk management involves four stages:
   » identification
   » quantification
   » managing/responding
   » monitoring/controlling.
6 Risk management in banking involves three key measures:
   » sensitivity
   » volatility
   » downside measures such as VaR.
7 Risk management strategies in banking include hedging, setting credit limits, having trading limits, and establishing risk management committees.
8 Failing to manage risks can have significant impacts on the organization and usually involves financial loss.
9 Effective risk management can be of great benefit because it allows an organization to navigate through the complexities and pitfalls it faces in the execution of its business activities.

NOTE

1 This case study is derived from an article that appeared in *Money Week*, August 3, 2001, p. 28.

The Evolution of Risk Management

The increasing complexity of organizations has necessitated effective risk management, but what else has led to its increased importance? Chapter 3 discusses:

» how increasing complexity has led to organizations managing more than just their financial risk;
» the impacts of human behavior, particularly in relation to over-commitment;
» the need for strong corporate governance that must entail the effective management of risk; and
» a timeline highlighting the notable events that led to the discipline of risk management.

". . . the serious study of risk began during the Renaissance, when people broke loose from the constraints of the past and subjected long held beliefs open to challenge . . ."

Peter Bernstein, economist and risk management guru

"The crash of 1929 and the economic crisis that followed led to major changes in bank regulation in the United States. The regulators focused on what is termed today as 'systemic risk' . . ."

Crouhy, Galai & Mark, risk management experts

"Escalation refers to a predicament where decision makers find themselves trapped in a losing course of action as a result of previous decisions. Costs are incurred; there is an opportunity to withdraw or to persist; and the consequences of withdrawal or persistence are uncertain. Typically, the response of such dilemmas is irrational persistence."

Helga Drummond, organizational psychologist and managing director of Feedback Change Consultancy

The discipline of risk management has emerged to become one of the most important competencies within the modern organization. The evolution of risk management is the result of many things, not least the development of numbering systems, mathematics, statistics, and most importantly probability. However, these alone do not explain why risk management as a discipline evolved into what it is today. Three aspects are explored in this chapter; the risks associated with organizational complexity, the need to guard against irrational decision-making and over-commitment, and the need to introduce effective corporate governance and controls.

THE RISE OF CORPORATE COMPLEXITY

As the sophistication of organizations grew, so did the types and complexity of the risks they faced. Over time, they realized that an increasing number of risks they faced were not purely financial in nature and many were outside of their direct control. This was particularly true as organizations became reliant on others to provide the goods and services they needed to create the products for their ultimate consumers. Initially starting with financial risk, other disciplines emerged. For example, the need to build complex products, particularly within the aerospace industry, saw the emergence of project management. At the time (1950s), project management was designed to manage the significant financial and technical risks associated with constructing huge passenger aircraft. But, as the value of project management grew, organizations in every sector adopted the principles of project management to manage their change and product development activities. In the modern organization, up to 30% of activity is now project-based.

During the 1980s there were a number of high profile disasters including the Challenger space shuttle explosion, the failure of the Bank of New York's mainframe, the mis-selling of personal pensions in the UK, the power outages that affected the US Federal Reserve Bank, and the failure of hedge funds. Each served to highlight gaps in the management of risk and helped to define the newer discipline of operational risk management.

The impact of globalization has also increased the levels of risk that organizations face, particularly for transnational corporations that operate globally. The emergence of powerful nongovernmental organizations has brought into sharp relief the impacts of environmental and workforce exploitation. Multinational corporations soon learnt that it was essential to manage the downside risks of globalization more carefully. Chapter 5 will explore the issues associated with globalization in more detail and outline what these mean for the management of risk.

THE NEED TO GUARD AGAINST IRRATIONAL OVER-COMMITMENT

As well as the risks associated with organizational complexity, firms also have to deal with issues about individual responsibility and accountability. Because risks have become more complex and their consequences more significant, people have become less willing to raise risks early enough to allow them to be effectively managed. The real danger here is that the person managing the risk fails to control it, making it increasingly harder to conceal and almost impossible to deal with. This type of problem is often found in investment banks when traders try to trade their way out of a loss. Many find it difficult to take a loss and instead hang onto losers. Unfortunately, a loss of 10% requires a gain of more than 11% to get even and a loss of 50% requires a gain of 100%. Therefore, without some kind of risk management mechanism such problems can, in extreme cases, lead to the failure of an entire bank as we saw with Nick Leeson and Barings. This problem is not unique to investment banks, of course. This process of over-committing to a failing position (or to a series of wrong decisions) is known as escalation.

The foundation of escalation lies in the irrational behaviors of individuals, which can be viewed at three distinct levels – the individual, the group, and the senior executive. This extra level has been included because the positional power of the senior executive allows the intensity of the irrational behaviors to be amplified. Although it can be argued that the behaviors identified at this level are equally applicable to the individual level, it is power that makes these behaviors more damaging.

Individual behavior

» *Availability error*. The most recent material is "available." Previous knowledge and data are lost in the immediacy of the event. Not surprisingly, this type of irrational behavior is often stimulated by dramatic events.

» *Halo effect*. The tendency to see all personal attributes consistently. For example, a good sportsman is expected to be a good businessman, father, indeed good at everything. This can equally work in the reverse, where someone is classed as being a general all-round poor performer.

» *Primacy error*. Beliefs formed by first impressions, with later evidence interpreted in light of these initial impressions. The adage "first impression counts" is applicable here. If powerful, primacy error can generate positive or negative halo effects very early on within a relationship.

» *Conformity error*. Individual conformance to the behavior of others, whether they know they are making a mistake by doing so, or whether they are unaware both of their mistake and of the social pressure that has induced them to make it.

Group behavior

» *Groups*. Where group members' attitudes are biased in one direction, the interaction of the group will tend to increase this bias because of the need to be valued and suppress criticism. Engaging in a common task only decreases hostility between groups if the outcome is successful. Where it is not, blame is passed from one group to the other, with any existing divisions widening.

» *Stereotypes*. Stereotypes are convenient tools for assessing an individual who belongs to a group. As a result, rather than being expected to act individually, a member of a group is expected to conform to the stereotypical behavior of the entire group. Therefore, no attempt is made at assessing an individual's behavior in isolation from the rest of the group. Stereotypes tend to be self-fulfilling because of both primacy and availability errors.

Senior executive behavior

» *Public decisions*. Public decisions are more likely to be executed than those taken privately. In general, people do not want to lose face, especially in public.

» *Misplaced consistency*. Someone who has embarked on a course of action may feel they must continue to justify their initial decision. People who have made a sacrifice – time, effort, or money – in order to do something, tend to go on doing it even when they stand to lose more than they could gain by continuing. There is always the hope that the situation can be retrieved.

» *Ignoring the evidence*. People tend to seek confirmation of their current hypothesis whereas they should be trying to disconfirm it. In general, there is a refusal to look for contradictory evidence or, indeed, believe or act upon it if it is brought to one's attention.

» *Distorting the evidence*. Evidence favoring a belief will strengthen the belief whilst contradictory evidence is ignored. As a result, the belief remains intact. Therefore, when faced with evidence that is contrary to a particular viewpoint, it will be distorted and dismissed as being irrelevant or inapplicable. Where the evidence is partially correct, it will be distorted to emphasize the positive aspects over the negative.

Organizations would do well to familiarize themselves with these behaviors and their links to risk. For example, if we look at the behavior of Nick Leeson during the period when he was trading derivatives on behalf of Barings, it is clear (from hindsight) that he was acting irrationally. He displayed all of the individual behaviors outlined above. But, in order for the over-commitment to reach the levels that it did, the team in which Leeson was working also had to act irrationally. And, in order for him to bet the bank, his managers back in London were guilty of misplaced consistency and ignoring the evidence. The subsequent collapse of Barings was ultimately the result of the poor management of risk, which itself was the result of over-commitment and its associated irrational behaviors. As this is written, the liability of the bank's auditors is still unresolved.

THE NEED FOR CORPORATE GOVERNANCE AND RISK CONTROL STANDARDS

With increased complexity and the dangers of irrational behavior, risks can soon spiral out of control. Therefore, in order to protect shareholders, workers, and investors from unnecessary risks, regulation has been imposed on publicly quoted companies (where the implications of poor risk management are largest). Regulation is ultimately designed to protect the corporation's shareholders, investors, and creditors from the risk of financial collapse. And although regulation has long been the preserve of the financial institution, such as investment banks, the deregulation of many industries, such as utilities, telecommunications, and transportation, has led to increasing levels of regulation. This is important because it counters the risks that organizations take in the pursuit of profits and it also protects against the systemic risks of market failure.

The majority of regulation has been aimed at the board of directors, who by virtue of their position control the destiny of the organization and the money of its investors. Such regulation has called for more discipline and control in three principal areas: effectiveness and efficiency of operations; reliability of financial reporting; and compliance with laws and regulation. In particular, the 1990s has seen an increased level of interest in establishing proper standards for control and risk management. Typical of these are:[1]

» COSO (USA). This was born out of the Treadway Commission report of 1987 that recommended the creation of an integrated and consistent set of internal controls and definitions. Following the report, a task force was established under the auspices of the Committee of Sponsoring Organizations of the Treadway Commission (COSO) to review the then available literature on internal control. The result of this was a series of definitions and management responsibilities associated with internal control systems. COSO stated that control systems should contain five interrelated components: the control environment itself; risk assessment; control activities; information and communication; and monitoring.

» Cadbury (UK). The Cadbury report made recommendations on corporate governance requirements. Unsurprisingly, these were very similar to the COSO recommendations, except in this instance they became mandatory rather than voluntary. And, since 1995, the boards of directors of listed companies have been required to review the effectiveness of their internal financial controls. This was followed in 1998 with a combined code issued by the London Stock Exchange which linked the recommendations from Cadbury with directors' roles and responsibilities.

» CoCo (Canada). In 1995 the Criteria of Control Board (CoCo) of the Canadian Institute of Chartered Accountants published the document *Guidance on Control*. This described 20 criteria for control against which the board of directors could assess themselves. The criteria were grouped under four headings: purpose; commitment; capability; and monitoring and learning.

» Turnbull (UK). The principal aim of Turnbull was to ensure that the management of risk within corporations was an ongoing process, rather than a one-off exercise at the end of each financial year. The guidance offered by Turnbull was more expansive than Cadbury in that it covered business, operational, and compliance controls, as well as financial control. More importantly, it linked the management of risk to the achievement of business objectives.

» CoBiT (International). The Control Objectives for Information and Related Technologies (CoBiT) attempts to set a general foundation for controlling IT both in terms of its security and general controls. The model recognizes the issues associated with the increasing dependency on IT for the effective operation of organizations and the risks that this presents. The CoBiT model has control objectives across five areas: planning and organization; acquisition and implementation; delivery; support; and monitoring. Within these five domains there are 34 control processes.

Each of these standards has ensured that boards of directors actively focus on the risks they take on behalf of their investors. They also begin to establish an appropriate risk management culture. Ultimately they protect investors and other company stakeholders from the worst excesses of corporate greed and incompetence.

TIMELINE

The following timeline highlights the most notable events that have led to the creation of the discipline we now call risk management.

- » **500**: Hindus develop the numbering system we use today.
- » **1200**: Hindu-Arabic numbering system reaches the West.
- » **1494**: Franciscan Monk Luca Paccioli publishes *Summa de arithmetica geometria et proportionalita* (very great abstraction and subtlety of mathematics), which introduces the concept of double-entry bookkeeping.
- » **1545**: Girolamo Cardano publishes *Ars Magna* (The Great Art), the first work to concentrate on algebra. He also publishes *Liber de Ludo Aleae* (Book on Games of Chance), which develops the statistical principles of probability.
- » **1657**: Huygens publishes a book on probability.
- » **1662**: Port-Royal monastery publishes *Logic*, which discusses philosophy and probability. The last four chapters of the book are dedicated to probability and include a description of a game in which 10 players risk one coin in the hope of winning the coins of the others.
- » **c1670**: John Gruant publishes a distribution of life expectancy from ages 6 to 76 that provides the inspiration for the UK's Central Statistical Office.
- » **1675**: Emergence of coffee houses in the City of London, which were used to swap news and information about sailing times, weather conditions and such like for merchant shipping.
- » **1693**: Edmund Halley publishes *Transactions*, in which he calculates annuity rates based on life expectancy. This will form the basis for the future life insurance industry.

» **1696**: Edward Lloyd launches the Lloyd's list, which contained details on the arrivals and departures of ships, and conditions abroad and at sea. The list was later expanded to include daily information on stock prices, foreign markets, and high water times at London Bridge.

» **1733**: Abraham De Moivre publishes *Doctrine of Chances*, which introduces the normal distribution (bell curve) which allowed him to calculate the dispersion about the mean of a set of observations (the standard deviation). This provided the basis of the assessment of an event's probability.

» **1738**: Daniel Bernouilli publishes a paper that discusses the new theory on the measurement of risk.

» **1801**: Carl Friedrich Gauss publishes *Disquisitiones Arithmeticae*, which discusses the theory of numbers.

» **1820–53**: Lambert Quetelet publishes three books on probability.

» **1933**: Glass-Steagall Act separates commercial banking from investment banking activities.

» **1936**: John Maynard Keynes publishes the *General Theory of Employment, Interest and Money*.

» **1952**: Portfolio selection revolutionizes the process of investment management by elevating risk to equal importance with expected return.

» **1960**: James Tobin and Bill Sharpe design the Capital Asset Pricing Model (CAPM).

» **1972**: The Mercantile Exchange in Chicago creates the International Money Market, specializing in foreign currency futures and options on futures on major currencies.

» **1982**: Options on fixed income securities introduced.

» **1990**: Equity index swaps introduced.

» **1992**: COSO and Cadbury control standards introduced; differential swaps introduced.

» **1996**: CoBiT control standard introduced.

BUBBLES, BLACK HOLES AND SCANDALS – WHAT HAPPENS WHEN NO ONE MANAGES RISK[2]

» **1637**: The bursting of the tulip bubble. When the market for tulips collapsed, the price of bulbs had risen 5900%. Investors lost everything they owned.
» **1720**: The bursting of the South Sea Bubble. A company without any track record or assets was able to convince investors to sell their holdings in the worthless Pacific Territories at higher and higher prices. When the bubble eventually burst, it took over 100 years for the London Stock Market to recover.
» **1929**: Wall Street Crash.
» **1963**: Salad oil scandal. American Express managed to lose an amount equivalent to its net value when it believed that financier Tony De Angelis had huge amounts of salad oil stored in New Jersey refineries when in fact he hadn't.
» **1979**: US businesses lose $1bn as a result of the Iranian revolution and the overthrow of the Shah.
» **1994**: Kidder Peabody Fiasco. Joseph Jett was accused of generating $350mn in phantom profits between 1991 and 1994.
» **1995**: Nick Leeson brought down Barings bank after he managed to lose $1.3bn on derivatives. The bank was later sold to ING for £1.
» **1996**: Sumitomo copper scandal. A trader was accused of conducting unauthorized trades over 10 years, losing $1.8bn.
» **1997**: NatWest Markets discovers a £50mn hole in its options trading book.
» **1998**: Failure of the Long-Term Capital Management hedge fund that almost brought down the global finance system.
» **2001**: The bursting of the dotcom bubble wiped billions off share prices as it was realized that the new economy was not that new at all.

KEY LEARNING POINTS
Evolution of risk management

1 Risk management as a discipline has emerged in response to the increasing complexity of the business environment.

2 People are inherently irrational and will prefer to hide and cover up their errors than own up and tackle them. When it comes to risks this leads to them going underground and escalating out of control.

3 Irrational behaviors that underpin escalation are grouped into three categories:
   » individual
   » group
   » senior executive.

4 Regulation has become an essential mechanism for protecting a company's investors and stakeholders from the risks they take.

5 Regulation has called on boards of directors to control and manage their risks. Examples include:
   » COSO
   » Turnbull
   » CoBiT
   » Cadbury.

NOTES

1 These summaries were drawn from the following Website: http://www.oprisk.freeserve.co.uk/Standards.htm
2 Cagan, P. (1999) "Risk financial management sources." *Econtent*, December.

The E-Dimension

The Internet has resulted in a whole tranche of new risks that have to be managed. This chapter discusses:

» the risks associated with electronic mail; and
» the major risks associated with internet ventures, including the "me-too" risk, the risk of failing to deliver a robust product, the risks of poor data currency, the risks of online fraud and the risks of security breaches and unauthorized access.

"E-mail may be a revolutionary method of communication but it is an insecure medium and many employees and employers are still unsure about where they stand when it comes to the legal implications."

Wendy Ledger, financial journalist

"Already, newspapers and trade journals regularly document the exploits of hackers, phreakers, and crackers using the Internet to commit a wide range of computer frauds and crimes, computer-related crimes, and to support other criminal behaviour. Many people from common users at home to corporate managers are concerned about the risks they run when they use the I-way.'

William Boni, leader, PricewaterhouseCoopers information protection practice and Dr Gerald Kovacich, high tech crime expert

NEW CHANNEL, NEW DANGER

The electronic channel has long been heralded as the next business innovation. And in response, organizations have rushed headlong into embracing e-commerce, opening up their business to the Internet and providing their staff with access to external e-mail. It is ironic, therefore, that the electronic dimension also presents significant risk.

THE RISKS OF E-MAIL

E-mail and the Internet have become essential business tools. But despite their utility, they pose an additional overhead in the management of risk. E-mail is an inherently insecure method of communication and is often treated far more casually than more formal methods of communication. When using e-mail, most employees tend to express opinions about their company, colleagues, and clients in a way they would never do using other media such as letters or faxes. And, unlike paper-based communication, e-mail can reach people who were not intended to receive it using such functions as blind copying, forwarding, and global address books.

There have been plenty of examples where statements made in an e-mail have resulted in embarrassment and, in extreme cases, litigation. Organizations need to be aware that if an e-mail is considered to be offensive, if it contains copyrighted material or confidential information, legal action can be taken against them. Unfortunately, organizations cannot intercept the e-mails of their employees despite the fact that they are liable for their content. Such things as the Human Rights Act, the UK's Data Protection Act, and more recently the Regulation of Investigatory Powers Act all serve to protect the employee and not the employer.

THE RISKS WITH THE INTERNET

Just as with e-mail, there are some inherent risks associated with the Internet. These fall into five broad categories: the risks associated with the "me-too" effect; the risk of failing to deliver a robust Website and associated services; the risk of poor data currency; the risks of online fraud; and the risk of security breaches.

The "me-too" risk

When the Internet became the next big thing, organizations rushed headlong into creating a Web presence, usually by developing an Internet equivalent of their bricks-and-mortar-based business. Many, it has to be said, felt that they had little choice but to respond to the emergence of the dotcom businesses who it was believed would steal their market share.

Unfortunately, the bursting of the dotcom bubble, coupled with the general reticence of people to conduct their business online, meant that most of this investment was wasted. A good example of this was the Internet banking rush that resulted in many banks investing hundreds of millions only to find there were not enough customers to justify their outlay. For example, in late October 2000, Allied Irish Bank became the largest European bank to scale back its online ambitions and plans for an Internet-only bank. It was joined by Japan's Sanwa Bank, which abandoned its ¥17bn online bank in favor of adding Internet banking to its other services. These and other banks have come to realize that there are too many cyberbanks chasing too few customers.[1]

Many others suffered financial loss; the venture capitalist, the private investors, and those people who bet their careers on the get rich quick dotcom bonanza. Had more care been exercised and the business risks managed, fewer would have suffered loss. As we will see in Chapters 6 and 7, adopting new and disruptive technologies requires the careful management of risk not the rash approach of the dotcoms.

LOSING OUT ON THE INTERNET BOOM[2]

CityReach International, the owner of eight Internet data centers in Europe, went into administration in August 2001, less than a year after it raised $155mn in funding. The company blamed poor take-up of its Web hosting and co-location services for large companies. The failure was due to too many data center service-based companies chasing too few customers. A very similar story to the Internet banks. The company had spent $180mn opening centers in London, Amsterdam, Budapest, Stockholm, and Paris.

The risk of failing to deliver a robust product

The early adopters of the Internet believed that new sites, products, and services could be launched rapidly and that the old rules of managing the risks associated with any new venture could be ignored. Most sites went live untested as organizations rushed to be first to market.[3] It should be remembered that testing new software systems and products has always been a time-consuming affair, and within a Web environment it has become more so because the environment is now part of the testing problem. The application may be simpler, but the environment in which they operate is not.[4] Testing costs in new economy projects are typically determined by the size and complexity of the application, the size and complexity of the architecture, the complexity of the user interface, and the knowledge and expertise of the user. Testing can soon become both time-consuming and costly.

Unfortunately, the comprehensive testing needs of Web-based applications is lost on most organizations, and according to one recent survey, two-thirds do not believe it is any different from standard system testing. But in the new economy the impact of poor software has the capacity to go global in a very short space of time, and with the market space becoming increasingly crowded, customers will find it easier to go elsewhere if the product or service fails.

It is also clear that new economy software products and systems are just as liable to crash as their old economy counterparts. For example:

» In June 1999 auction site eBay suffered a 22-hour crash; the longest, but not last in a series of damaging outages. In its struggle to keep up with demand, the auction site had failed to make a standard software fix to a known bug in its operating system. As a result, nearly $5bn was wiped from its market value.

» In August 1999, hundreds of customers of the UK retailer Tesco were cut off from the supermarket's Internet shopping service for over a week when the software failed. People who had become dependent on the software found that it repeatedly failed after it had been upgraded.

Managing the technical risks associated with the Internet must be carefully considered both during development and once operational. As stated earlier, it is difficult to cover up a major software glitch when it is visible to literally the entire world.

The risks of poor data currency

Managing information – in its widest sense – is a key part to any business, but in a Web-based environment it is even more important. And yet, according to a recent survey by the UK's National Opinion Poll, 77% of organizations publish out-of-date information on their Websites and 41% believed that information was duplicated across their sites. This is despite 83% claiming that their Websites are important business tools.[5] If customers depend on the site having up-to-date information about your products and services, and this proves not to be the case, they will soon lose interest. According to a recent review in the *Financial Times*, the two most important success factors in Website design are the ability to keep the site up-to-date and having useful content and information. The same article suggested that these two aspects also prove to be the most difficult to get right.[6]

The risks of online fraud

Although the electronic channel has created enormous opportunities to sell products globally, it has also exposed Web merchants to new risks, particularly those associated with fraud. Although it is difficult to assess the full extend of Internet fraud, it is believed that it represents approximately 0.9% of online transactions. The costs to the merchant can be significant and are not just related to the loss of the goods secured fraudulently. According to ClearCommerce, costs fall into five areas.[7]

» *Cost of goods sold*. As it will be unlikely that any goods will be recovered in the case of fraud, their value has to be written off. The impact will be greatest for low margin merchants. And as a large percentage of e-commerce sites are low margin (because they have to undercut high street prices to tempt people away from their bricks-and-mortar equivalent) this affects most sites.

» *Shipping costs*. Fraudsters usually ask for high priority shipping, as this allows them to complete their transaction as quickly as possible and avoid detection. And because shipping is usually bundled in with the order price, this too will have to be written off.

» *Card association fee*. Card issuers such as Visa and MasterCard penalize merchants for generating excessive chargebacks. If a merchant exceeds chargeback rates for any three-month period they are penalized with a $25 fee for every chargeback. And this fee increases up to $100 if the level is not controlled by the merchant in the following months. Those with excessive chargeback can be fined between $5500 and $100,000 per month and in extreme cases the card issuer will terminate the service agreement, thereby preventing the merchant from conducting its business over the Internet.

» *Bank fees*. Banks charge processing fees ranging from $10 to $25 for every chargeback.

» *Administration costs*. On average, each chargeback requires up to two hours of administration.

Many online traders underestimate the level of fraud they can experience, especially when they are setting up their Websites. Because fraud increases with the level of traffic, newly formed Web merchants tend to ignore the importance of security and pay a heavy price.

The risks of security breaches and unauthorized access

The risks associated with the electronic channel are not restricted to Internet merchants, as any organization that is connected to the Internet is at risk from hackers and criminals accessing their systems. According to a 1998 PricewaterhouseCoopers and *Information Week* security survey of over 1600 management information systems officials from over 40 countries, nearly 73% had experienced security breaches. Some had lost $10mn or more in single incidents.[8] For some organizations, it is the number of breaches themselves that is an even bigger concern. A study by War Room Research suggested that more than 50% of the companies they surveyed had experienced more than 30 system penetrations during a 12 month period and 60% reported losing $200,000 or more from each intrusion.[9]

The impacts of viruses should also not be underestimated. The latest to hit organizations around the world was the Code Red virus that defaced Web pages, disrupted e-mail, hampered online commerce, and even forced computers to dial up the White House. The virus began replicating on July 19, 2001 and within nine hours had infected 250,000 systems. In response, the Pentagon shut down computer systems to assess its vulnerability and Microsoft had to issue a patch to its Windows 2000 and Windows NT operating systems to block the worm virus. The cost to businesses around the world ran into millions, if not billions.

The threats posed by the electronic channel are, of course, not always external. Disgruntled employees can wreak enormous damage when they hack into computer systems, plant viruses, and delete essential corporate data. This type of risk tends to rise during economic downturns when staff lose their jobs. For example, a 56-year-old systems administrator fired from his $186,000 job at a New Jersey chemical firm recently admitted to causing $20mn of damage.[10] The man concerned used another employee's password to tap into the company's computer system through an Internet connection in his home to delete critical inventory and personnel files. In another case, an IT expert was accused of planting a computer time bomb in his former employer's network which permanently erased the company's manufacturing program, causing $10mn in damage. According to the Federal Bureau of Investigation and the Company Security Institute, such attacks led to a loss of $378mn in 2000.

A recent survey points to the scale and reach of cybercrime.[11]

» Two-thirds of the respondents had experienced serious incidents in the past year including hacking, virus attacks, and credit card fraud.
» The main threat comes from external hackers, former employees, and organized crime.
» Current employees account for 11% of the crimes.

» Only 32% of companies believe that business-to-consumer transactions are safe, compared to 53% of business-to-business transactions.

KEY LEARNING POINTS
The e-dimension

1 The electronic channel has widened the nature of risk for most organizations.
2 E-mail can cause major problems for organizations through the ability to transmit illegal, offensive, and company-sensitive information at the touch of a button.
3 The risks associated with the electronic channel fall into five main categories:
   » me-too;
   » failure to deliver a robust product;
   » poor data currency and integrity;
   » online fraud; and
   » security breaches and unauthorized access.
4 Risks associated with the electronic channel are not restricted to external agents. Employees are also capable of causing significant financial loss when they sabotage systems and data.

NOTES

1 Mackintosh, J. (2000) "How banking on the Internet has become a fallen icon." *Financial Times*, October 27, p. 29.
2 Grande, C. (2001) "CityReach joins Internet failures." *Financial Times*, August 29.
3 Vowler, J. (2000) "Testing time for e-commerce." *Computer Weekly*, October 19, p. 70.
4 Sneed, H. & Goschl, S. (2000) "Testing software of Internet applications." *Focus Review*, Volume 1, Issue 1.
5 Vowler, J. (2000) "Testing time for e-commerce." *Computer Weekly*, October 19, p. 70.
6 "Key criteria for website success." *Financial Times*, July 18, 2001, Section II.

7 ClearCommerce white paper. Fraud prevention guide.
8 Boni, W. & Kovacich, G. (1999) *I-Way Robbery: Crime on the Internet*. Butterworth-Heinemann, Woburn, MA, p. 28.
9 *Ibid.*, p. 28.
10 Alexander, G. (2001) "Hacking by sacked staff costs US firms billions." *Sunday Times*, August 5, p. 3.
11 Barker, T. (2001) "Cybercrime is stifling e-business, warns CBI." *Financial Times*, August 23.

The Global Dimension

Globalization has allowed organizations to extend their corporate reach around the world. It has provided a rich source of human capital which is cheaper than in the industrialized world. However, the combination of the Internet and an increased awareness of global issues has raised new risks. This chapter outlines:

» the types of risks transnational corporations face;
» the importance of nongovernmental organizations;
» best practice: Levi Strauss;
» the increased level of country risk; and
» the risks imposed when the economic cycles of major trading nations coincide.

". . . many non-governmental organizations have realised that the quickest way to get results is to go directly after companies by targeting their customers, their investors or both."

Financial Times

"Good reputation is a company asset. Good reputations are built up over years and take years to repair, but can be destroyed overnight."

Peter Schwartz, scenario planning expert and author, and Blair Gibb, international trade specialist and poet

The process of globalization started during the 1960s with the emergence of multinational and transnational corporations that coincided with the expansion of international trade following the Second World War. During the 1970s a number of factors came together that molded globalization into what we know today. These were:[1]

» the internationalizing of capital markets;
» the expansion of international securities investment and bank lending;
» the increasing sophistication of information technology used within commerce;
» the emergence of the Internet;
» the economic competition from Japan;
» the General Agreement on Tariffs and Trade of 1947;
» the reduction in state control and the subsequent rise in deregulation; and
» the oil crisis.

Each of these factors led governments and organizations to consider how they could remain competitive in a commercial environment with fewer controls and increased competition. Many corporations responded by merging with, or acquiring, other organizations that were better placed to deliver a truly global service. Others sought out the cheapest labor with which to manufacture their goods, leading to a massive reduction in the manufacturing bases of the industrialized world as the work was transferred to the cheaper economies of the Far East, Central Asia, and, more recently, China.

With further advances in technology since the 1970s, globalization has increasingly allowed the transfer of knowledge around the world. And with the emerging economies of Asia providing a ready source of well-educated cheap labor, corporations are beginning to source their knowledge workers from overseas rather than at home. In addition, as competition hots up, corporations are having to develop more sophisticated knowledge-based products and services in order to compete within the global market. Not unexpectedly, globalization has significantly increased the number of transnational corporations that have grown steadily from 7000 in 1975 to 37,000 in 1994. And, according to Peter Schwartz and Blair Gibb, authors of *When Good Companies Do Bad Things*, globalization has changed not only industry structures but also communication networks and markets. In particular, business behavior and its effects now reach a worldwide audience. This introduces new risks that have to be managed.

THE RISKS OF GOING GLOBAL

Until recently, globalization has offered plenty of upside and not too much downside. Cheap labor has allowed corporations to produce their goods with much lower input costs, thereby allowing them to increase margins. In addition, many developing and Far Eastern countries have offered preferential tax rates and government support to persuade major manufacturers and businesses to site in their countries. However, with the advent of the Internet and the increased interest in the environment and the exploitation of developing nations' workforces, transnational corporations are now at risk from pressure groups and boycotts that can seriously hit their bottom line and do untold damage to their brand. Here are some examples.[2]

» In September 2000, protesters from the Campaign to Eliminate Conflict Diamonds set up pickets outside Cartier on 5th Avenue, New York. Shoppers were confronted by images from the civil war in Sierra Leone with captions "Did your diamonds do this?" The demonstration was reinforced by primetime television adverts aimed at forcing the US diamond industry to support legislation to stem the flow of illegal diamonds, thereby eliminating one of the major sources of rebel funds. Within eight months the industry agreed to block the import of diamonds coming from war zones. The response from the jewelry business was vital if it was to preserve the image and integrity of the diamond as a symbol of love.

» In 2000 the William Casey Institute led a successful campaign to dissuade investors from an initial public offering by Petro-China, the Chinese oil company, which was active in Tibet and Sudan.

» In 1999 Home Depot, the world's largest retailer of timber products, agreed to stop buying wood cut from old-growth forests after the Rainforest Action Network and other environmental groups held a series of protests in front of their stores and ran an advertising campaign that denounced the company.

Similar actions have impacted other global organizations including Nike, Wal-Mart, Gap, and Shell. And behind many of these actions are nongovernmental organizations (NGOs), which have emerged to fill the void left by governments as they withdrew from setting the boundaries of corporate social responsibility. These organizations, which include Greenpeace and Amnesty International, have expanded in number and breadth over the last 20 years. There are now some 16,000 internationally recognized NGOs and a further 50,000 local equivalents operating in the developing nations.

The continued rise in NGOs means that organizations have to manage the risks from political, environmental, anticapitalist, and human rights activists as carefully as any other risks they face. In extreme cases these groups can cause major disruption, as we have witnessed with the anticapitalist demonstrations and riots that have coincided with the G-8 summits around the world. This pressure for more business and social responsibility often focuses around single issues and usually blows up very quickly once it captures the public's imagination. The fact that it takes corporations by surprise demonstrates the limited attention they pay to this type of risk. But it also reflects just how quickly pressure groups can mobilize themselves through a combination of the Internet and mobile telephony (as the UK saw during the fuel crisis at the end of 2000).

LEVI STRAUSS – THE GOOD CORPORATE CITIZEN[3]

Levi Strauss is one of the increasing number of global corporations that take social responsibility seriously. It uses the phrase *responsible commercial success* to describe its promise to shareholders. The firm understands the linkage between the values the business has in relation to corporate and social responsibility and its long-term success. These values are communicated to its entire staff through aspiration statements and documents that serve as a code of conduct. This code of conduct is tailored to individual functions. For example, the marketing code of conduct includes statements such as these.

» "Learn to embrace diversity."
» "Be responsible, not afraid."
» "Take the time to understand the difference between a portrayal and a stereotype."
» "Always judge the messaging of our advertising from the eyes of the consumers."

Levi Strauss actively monitors the implementation of its codes of conduct and enforces them through such things as requiring its local contractors to employ positive employment practices.

THE FINANCIAL RISKS OF GLOBALIZATION – INCREASED COUNTRY RISK

When business transactions occur across international borders they involve additional risks beyond those that are managed in a domestic setting. This is known as country risk and it arises because of the different business, economic, and political environments that exist around world. Although some form of country risk has always been present between trading partners, globalization has emphasized the imbalances. This means that, for those organizations that are transnational, the management of country risk is an increasingly important capability. There are six main categories to country risk.[4]

» *Economic risk*. This is the risk that the expected return on an investment held/made within a country is affected by changes in a country's economic structure or growth. Such risks arise from significant changes in fiscal and monetary policy, local recessions, and resource availability.

» *Transfer risk*. This arises from restrictions in capital movements imposed by foreign governments. Such restrictions can occur during times of difficult economic or trading conditions, such as during the Asian Crisis in the late 1990s, when some Asian governments imposed fixed exchange rates to minimize the impact of falling currency values.

» *Exchange risk*. This is the risk that there is a sudden change in the value of a country's currency. Such changes are usually associated with economic turmoil or speculative attacks by investors (as we saw when the UK joined and subsequently left the European Exchange Rate Mechanism in 1992). Risk can also arise when a country moves from a fixed to a floating exchange rate.

» *Location or neighborhood risk*. This in essence is where the problems of one country spill over to the next. This can happen in times of war (such as during the Gulf War and more recently in the Balkans) and regional economic difficulty (as we saw in Latin America in the 1980s, and Asia in the 1990s).

» *Sovereign risk*. This is the risk associated with the failure of the government to meet its loan obligations, as with the Russians' default in 1998.

» *Political risk*. This relates to the general political stability of the country that can change in times of regional wars, military coups, and civil war.

How country risk is managed depends very much on the nature of the relationship the organization has with the countries with which it trades. For example, if it has located a manufacturing plant in another country, the risk will be long-term and will require the organization to assess all aspects of the country's risk before the investment is made and for a long time after. In particular, political risks have to be carefully monitored in those parts of the world which have a history of instability. Country risk also varies with the type and nature of loans. Long-term loans to governments usually have low economic risk, but high exchange, sovereign, and political risks, whilst a short-term loan to a private entity is typically low risk apart from transfer risk.

THE HOUSE OF CARDS RISK – WHEN ECONOMIC CYCLES COINCIDE

Computerization has been the backbone of globalization. And in the process, it has revolutionized the production and supply of goods and services. It allows everything to be delivered when it is needed, through just in time manufacturing and mass customization, with no stocks and no idle capital. But such leanness can lead to significant problems when there is an investment slump, because there is no buffer to lessen the effects of the downturn. Recessions can now travel around the globe at Internet speed, and according to Anthony Hilton, the downside of globalization is globalized slump. For example, in the early part of 2001, we witnessed the rapid demise of telecommunications and technology businesses that were affected by the contraction of the US economy and the bursting of the dotcom bubble. Organizations could do little to manage their risk as shares plummeted, markets dried up, and income dropped. As this is written, the global economy shows little sign of recovery as it slides gently into recession.

KEY LEARNING POINTS
The global dimension

1 Globalization has exposed organizations to new forms of risk.
2 Companies that operate globally must concern themselves with their social and corporate responsibilities.
3 Those that fail to do so will face the wrath of campaigners and NGOs who will not cease until the organization has changed its attitude toward issues such as the environment and exploitation of their workforces in developing countries.
4 Country risk comprises:
    » economic risk;
    » transfer risk;
    » exchange risk;
    » location or neighborhood risk;

> » sovereign risk; and
> » political risk.
5 Although the global financial and economic system is efficient, there are systemic risks when one part of it fails.

NOTES

1 Jarvis, P. (2001) *Universities and Corporate Universities: The Higher Learning Industry in Global Society*. Kogan Page, London, p. 21; Hirst, P. & Thompson, P. (1996) *Globalisation in Question*. Blackwell, Oxford, p. 18.

2 Alden, R. (2001) "Brands feel the impact as activists target customers." *Financial Times*, July 18, p. 11.

3 Schwartz, P. & Gibb, B. (1999) *When Good Companies Do Bad Things: Responsibility and Risk in an Age of Globalization*. John Wiley & Sons, New York, pp. 92–3.

4 Meldrum, D. (2000) "Country Risk and Foreign Direct Investment." *Business Economics*, January.

The State of the Art

Succeeding at risk management is now a multidisciplinary skill. This means understanding and managing the broad range of risks that face the organization. This chapter discusses how best to respond. It includes:

» managing the risks of globalization;
» managing technical risks;
» managing the e-channel risks;
» managing the financial risks of an e-business, such as online fraud and unauthorized access;
» managing operational risks; and
» risk roles and responsibilities.

"As the pace of change continues to accelerate, many organizations are now finding that they can no longer afford to take a solely defensive attitude to risk. While control frameworks are a necessary first step in managing risk, many organizations now need to manage risk for strategic advantage, to improve customer satisfaction and increase shareholder value."

Chris Frost, Dave Allen, James Porter, and Phillip Bloodworth,
risk management consultants

"In the 1970s, techno-crimes such as computer fraud were rare ... Perpetrators generally were computer specialists ... After all they were the only ones who knew how to operate and use the technology ... In the 1980s, the type and frequency of techno-crimes changed due to the personal computer, telecommunications advancements and networking. The internal types of perpetrators were expanded ... During this period, the external threats began to grow ... In the 1990s and into the 21st century, international crime and frauds developed and will continue to develop, due to increased international networking."

William Boni, leader, PricewaterhouseCoopers information
protection practice and Dr Gerald Kovacich, high tech crime
expert

The effective management of risk requires a combination of process and procedures, support systems and clear roles and responsibilities. This chapter discusses the current best practice around all aspects of risk management.

MANAGING THE RISKS OF GLOBALIZATION

As we saw in Chapter 5, globalization presents new risks that can have significant impacts on the bottom line. It is clear that transnational corporations have had to become better at managing the risks associated with the environment, the exploitation (perceived or otherwise) of their workforce and their presence in countries with poor human rights or which are war-torn or corrupt. Peter Schwartz and Blair Gibb, authors of *When Good Companies Do Bad Things*, recommend the following actions as a way of reducing the risks of globalization.

» Think about the issues. Global organizations must spend time considering the wider implications of their actions. Many organizations believe this is too unclear and too ill-defined to bother about, concentrating instead on the more tangible aspects of their business. This lack of action tends to result in crisis management when issues arise. Asking difficult questions about their business and of their social responsibility are vital if they are to sensitize themselves to the risks and begin to manage them. This ultimately means adopting a wider perspective on risk and risk management and ensuring they understand the wider concerns about their business activities around the globe.

» Identify the stakeholders and develop a close working relationship with them. Working with nongovernmental organizations (NGOs) is one way to reduce risk. When working with the stakeholders it is important to do more homework by considering the types of questions they might need answers to. The simple advice here is to ask.

» Think in scenarios. Deep thinking about the future is important and if the wider stakeholder community is involved, these scenarios can be greatly enriched. Following the problems experienced in Nigeria during 1995, Shell now develops scenarios jointly with Amnesty International.

» Build and integrate new competencies around social and corporate responsibility.

CREATING STANDARDS FOR GLOBAL CITIZENSHIP

With the increasing impact of NGOs on global corporations, there has been a recognition that some basic standards need to be established to improve their relationships within the countries in which they operate. Such standards are designed to reduce the downside risks on the environment, the exploitation of labor, and ultimately the risks of direct action against them. Transnational corporations have realized that they have to manage their global stakeholders much more effectively than they have in the past.

The Caux Round Table (CRT) was set up in 1995 by a group of international business leaders to create and adopt a set of standards for conducting international business with a particular emphasis on social responsibility:

» to promote sustainable development;
» to promote human rights and democratic institutions wherever practicable;
» to collaborate with those in the community who are working to promote health and education; and
» to be a good corporate citizen.

As the number, sophistication, and influence of NGOs increase, transnational organizations would be very wise to engage them more actively. Peter Schwartz and Blair Gibb believe that the typical process through which an issue would be raised by the NGO would follow the pattern below.

» An activist within the NGO would raise an issue. This is likely to be specific to the organization concerned, such as we saw with Shell and the decommissioning of Brent Spar, or Starbucks and the livelihoods of their coffee growers. At this stage the issue will be internal to the NGO.
» The NGO would then begin a campaign to assess public reaction to the issue, which may be conducted in coalition with other groups. Its purpose is to determine the strength of reaction and hence whether the public will support it. In some cases the public will not show enough interest to take it further.
» When there is sufficient public support the NGO will engage government or international bodies to develop a policy and, where appropriate, a legal response.
» The NGO then becomes part of the monitoring process to ensure those transnational corporations affected are complying with the new policy or law.
» Ultimately the NGO becomes a resource to the transnational corporation, helping them define policy and gathering the local intelligence it needs to monitor its activities. The advantage of engaging the

NGO in this instance is that they often have established links with workforces, other environmental groups, and so on. This means that they can both highlight inconsistencies and areas of non-compliance that need to be addressed, but more importantly help to demonstrate the concern and positive actions of the transnational corporation they are helping.

As awareness of the environmental and social consequences of globalization increases, the risks that transnational corporations have to manage will become more complex. Therefore, actively engaging NGOs in the process of establishing appropriate business and social responsibility is an ideal way of managing this type of risk.

MANAGING TECHNICAL RISKS

With technology taking a significant role in the creation of new products, organizations have recognized that managing the risks of bringing a new technology product to market is an essential skill. A prime example of where this was not the case was the rush to join the Third Generation telecommunications bandwagon. Typical of the telecommunication companies that responded was BT, who spent billions to purchase licenses from the UK government, only to saddle itself with enormous debt, which it has subsequently had to eliminate by restructuring the company. BT is not alone, as many other companies around Europe are now writing off their investment as realism sets in around the technical viability and likely take-up. Lewis Branscomb and Philip Auerswald, authors of *Taking Technical Risks*, offer the following strategies for dealing with the combination of technical (product) failure and market failure when introducing new technology products.

» Obtain more cash at a given point in the future. Organizations with successful technological innovations focus on both the manufacture of their own proprietary products and some liquidity event that ensures their investors see a return on their investment. This includes initial public offerings that raise additional capital through the stock market. The capital raised is then used to continue product and business development as well as providing the venture capitalist with a return on their investment. This was a typical approach adopted by the dotcoms.

» Obtain the same cash inflows, but sooner. This usually involves establishing partnership deals with third parties.

» Reducing cash outflows. Because technical innovations can become money sinks, organizations can adopt a number of strategies to reduce the risks they face. They can enter into partnership deals (as above). They can delay product launch until the product is robust enough to reduce the market's acceptance. Although there is always a risk attached to any delay, the consequences of releasing an unreliable product can be worse, especially if it is being launched globally (such as through the Internet). Other strategies include adopting a risk-reward approach with backers, where the amount they receive as the return on their investment varies according to the level of risk they take. This is particularly useful if the backer is well known within the target market, as they can serve to reduce the level of market risk.

» Obtaining the same outflows, but later. Stage payments based upon technology performance allow the product and market risks to be managed more effectively. This is a common technique used by venture capitalists as a way of managing their financial risk, but is also a good method for managing the risks associated with product failure.

» Reducing the risks of cash inflows. Any product worth its salt should be capable of bringing in more money than was invested in it. It is a sad fact that this is often not the case. Therefore organizations must take a long hard look at the market risks before product development starts, during its development and prior to its launch. This can be achieved through market research and working closely with the ultimate customers of the product.

» Trickle-up rather than trickle-down product development. Many products are aimed at the high end of the market and tend to be very sophisticated, functionally rich, and as a consequence prone to failure. Also, when a complex product is launched, organizations then have to battle with the problem of making a cheaper, less complex variant for other markets. This can be difficult. The alternative strategy is to begin with a simple product and build its level of sophistication over time. In this way it is possible to iron out the major manufacturing and product glitches early on. The Japanese used this approach very successfully with the development of charged couple devices, which are now an integral part of every computer laptop. They followed a performance-enhancing process rather than a cost-reducing one.

MANAGING THE E-CHANNEL RISKS

As we discussed in Chapter 4, there are a number of risks that have emerged alongside the Internet. In particular, the risks associated with e-mail, electronic fraud, and system penetration require special attention from risk managers. All entail managing the financial risks associated with the actions of staff (in the case of e-mail), over-exuberance (in the case of developing an e-presence) and the actions of third parties (be they fraudsters or hackers).

E-mail risk management

According to Tarlo Lyons, a technologies and communications law firm, addressing the risks of e-mail requires that organizations establish clear policies on its use. They recommend that such policies should include:[1]

» banning the downloading of offensive material (usually pornography, 70% of which is downloaded between the hours of 9 and 5);
» prohibiting the sending of offensive e-mails (covering sexist, racist, abusive, and defamatory remarks);
» warning against the sending of commercially sensitive material. In ideal circumstances this should be encrypted first;
» ensuring that all e-mails have a suitable disclaimer, such as the following:

"The information transmitted is intended only for the person or entity to which it is addressed and may contain confidential and/or privileged material. Any review, retransmission, dissemination or other use of, or taking of any action in reliance upon, this information by persons or entities other than the intended recipient is prohibited. If you received this in error, please contact the sender and delete the material from any computer.

"Internet communications are not secure and therefore company x does not accept legal responsibility for the contents of this message. Any views or opinions presented are solely those of the author and do not necessarily represent those of company x."

» providing their employees with a clear indication of the circumstances under which e-mail will be monitored;
» making it clear that all e-mail attachments that originate from outside of the organization should be scanned for viruses before opening;
» warning staff that e-mails are classed as documents and can be used in a court of law; and
» notifying staff that a breach of the e-mail policy may lead to disciplinary action and possibly their dismissal.

Managing the financial risks of an e-business

According to Jeremy Kourdi, author of *New Economy Edge*, managing the risks associated with an online venture involves a number of strategies. First and foremost it is essential that the existing business processes are reviewed to understand how online developments will enhance profitability. Jumping into an e-business venture without thinking where the profits will come from was one of the principal reasons why so many dotcom companies failed. In the rush to establish an Internet presence, they failed to consider the business model. It is fair to say that the same applied to the venture capitalists that threw vast sums of money at anything that had an "e" in front of it.

Second, it is important to understand the key drivers in the e-business (revenue and cost). Third, a project plan for e-business should be developed which must include a full assessment of the costs and benefits of the venture and how it will provide an appropriate return on the investment. And finally, once operational, it is essential that key performance indicators are established that allow the organization to monitor the financial position of the e-business venture as it progresses. Key within this is to collect information that will allow the business leaders to make decisions about its direction and future.

Developing a reliable Internet presence

There is no doubt that projects in the "e" space have to be delivered faster than those in the old economy. As organizations rush to pursue Internet strategies and get connected, they have to be able to manage the increased speed, uncertainty, and risk that this presents. Speedier projects are needed because the market expects more, faster, and will not forgive tardiness on the part of organizations. E-projects involve degrees of uncertainty that most organizations are not used to. Whereas in the past, new technological territory could be forged by the pioneers, the new economy dictates that all organizations respond because if they don't, the financial markets will penalize them. This exposes those organizations that would have traditionally waited until the technology matured before taking action, to new risks. The organization needs to adopt the following strategies to ensure that they deliver an end product that their customers will use.

» Maintain the strategic perspective. The uncertainty of the electronic market has been made particularly evident over 2000–2001. This has made it clear that there is an increasing need to maintain a strategic perspective throughout the project to ensure that, when the strategy changes, the project changes with it or is terminated (for the right reasons). This helps to guard against over-commitment (see Chapter 3).

» Accept that we have no metrics. Organizations are notorious for failing to collect metrics on which they can base a future project's estimates. With the new economy, this has just got much harder, especially when we consider the implications of testing. In accepting that there are no metrics, and that there unlikely to be any for the foreseeable future, organizations must adopt a more flexible approach to software development and funding. This means collecting metrics as the project is executed, and learning from the experience.

» Build in small chunks – rapidly. Techniques such as rapid application development allow software products to be built in this way. Adopting the small project delivery model is appropriate for e-projects because of the difficulties of having no metrics, plus dealing with the uncertain nature of the markets. The small project delivery model allows the organizations to limit the likelihood of over-commitment and to make adjustments to the project in light of changes in strategy. Nimble projects are the order of the day and are essential in the management of the financial risks associated with them.

» Never compromise on testing. Be warned, failing to test Internet applications thoroughly can be highly damaging because Websites interact directly with the customer, and if they fail to live up to expectation, customers will abandon you. Failure can be very public.

Online fraud

When dealing with the risks of online fraud, merchants need to recognize the warning signs and then check the sale to assess whether it is a genuine aberration or a deliberate attempt to defraud the company of its services. According to ClearCommerce, the following warning signs have been consistently associated with cases of Internet fraud.

» Larger than normal orders. Is the order too good to be true? Online fraudsters will spend a large amount of money in a short space of time to maximize their return before the stolen credit card they are using is stopped.
» Orders containing more than one of the same item. Online fraudsters will usually buy multiple copies of the same item to onward sell. Similarly, multiple orders on the same credit card over a short space of time is equally suspicious.
» Urgent orders. Goods shipped using guaranteed next day delivery is one way that the online fraudster can ensure they get their goods as soon as possible and before any action can be taken to stop them.
» Shipping orders to an address other than the billing address. In general, the further away the shipping address is from the billing address, the greater the risk of fraud. However, fraudsters will sometimes ask the order to be shipped to the same address as the billing address and then, once the order has been dispatched, contact the shipping company to change the delivery address.

Unauthorized access

Understanding and managing the risks associated with unauthorized access to corporate computers is essential, especially with the increased connectivity that has occurred with globalization. Assessing the threat is the first step to take, and this involves two elements. The first is to understand the types of threats, which include hackers, phreakers, vendor/suppliers, ex-employees, business rivals, foreign government agents, customers, subcontractors, terrorists, and so on. The second is to assess the motivations of the threat by analyzing why they would want to hack into your computers. Just as there are a number of potential threats, so there are many motives. Key ones include former employees exacting revenge, competitors wanting to steal important corporate information, environmental activists wanting to discredit the organization, and political activists wishing to spoil or destroy Websites or corrupt information systems (such as we saw with the Code Red virus in summer 2001– see Chapter 4).

Once the basic source of the threat and their motive are assessed, it is then necessary to determine how they will attempt to gain access. Those attempting to gain unauthorized access tend to follow a similar route: they research their target, they identify the vulnerabilities, and they then use basic software tools to gain access. Knowing this allows the organization to assess their vulnerabilities and begin to eliminate them. When it comes to establishing basic protection, William Boni and Gerald Kovacich, authors of *I-Way Robbery*, recommend the following.

» *Administrative security*. This should include establishing the basic rules for Internet use and training all staff in its application.
» *Physical security*. This should include the creation of standards for all systems that are connected to the Internet. This extends to hardware, software, and networks. At the same time it is necessary to restrict access to security systems such as firewalls to those charged with their maintenance.
» *Operational security*. Underwriting the security of the organization's systems and data is never easy because of the access people have to the Internet. However, limiting the number of computers that have access to the Internet and restricting the sites that can be visited can provide some basic protection. This will require those sites that are not directly associated with business to be blocked. In addition, custom e-mail and file transfer filters that can allow the organization to identify access to insecure sites, such as USENET, can be helpful, or where they are transferring sensitive information. However, all organizations should be aware of the legal consequences of monitoring and intercepting e-mail. Because of this, it is better to have a clear policy that outlines the potential risks and how employees should respond.

» *Other security measures*. These include establishing an internal computer forensics capability to gather evidence and intelligence from internal systems in order to bring the perpetrators (whether internal or external) to justice. In addition, it is advisable to implement intrusion detection software on critical systems, compartmentalize internal networks, and enhance the authentication process.

MANAGING OPERATIONAL RISKS

According to the Risk Management Association, effective operational risk management requires organizations to establish a framework that consists of a set of integrated processes, tools, and mitigation strategies. Such a framework has six components to it.

1 *Strategy*. Understanding the strategy and objectives of the organization together with the goals of individual business units allows strategic risks to be identified. More importantly, however, it allows the organization to identify where the opportunities lie and what operational risks the organization will need to take in order to realize them. This establishes the organization's risk appetite.

2 *Risk policies*. Because operational risk touches on all areas of the organization, it is essential that policies be established to communicate the organization's approach to operational risk management. Such policies should provide a definition of what operational risk is, describe and define roles and responsibilities, and outline how the organization intends to manage the operational risks it faces.

3 *Risk management process*. This process should address how risks are identified, the types of operational controls that need to be in place, how risks will be measured and tracked, and what level of reporting is required.

4 *Risk mitigation*. This should identify the generic risk mitigation mechanisms open to the organization, such as business continuity planning, IT security, and compliance.

5 *Operations management*. For operational risk to be appropriately managed, it is essential that its management be embedded in all key operational activities, processes, and systems.

6 *Culture*. This is necessary to ensure the whole organization manages the balance between risk and opportunity.

RISK ROLES AND RESPONSIBILITIES

Organizations need to ensure that responsibilities for risk management are clearly defined throughout the enterprise. The Institute of Internal Auditors Research Foundation[2] offers the following advice on where responsibility lies for risk management (with some additions).

» The chief executive:
  » drives the focus on risk management throughout the whole organization;
  » is ultimately responsible and accountable for all risks that affect the viability and profitability of the organization; and
  » must understand the extent of the organization's most significant risks and ensure they are managed.
» The chief financial officer:
  » is responsible for all financial risk management activities;
  » acts on behalf of the chief executive in implementing a suitable risk management architecture; and
  » is responsible for maintaining an effective balance between risk and opportunity.
» The chief risk officer:
  » works with the organization to implement the risk architecture through which all risks will be managed;
  » ensures the risk architecture is suitably maintained and updated when required; and
  » monitors risk on an ongoing basis and manages and reports on the organization's risk profile.
» The internal audit:
  » is operationally responsible for the continuous assessment of risk within the organization. This is usually conducted through a series of rolling audits to ensure all operating units are managing risk appropriately; and
  » provides advice and guidance on matters of risk across all operating divisions.
» Project and program managers:
  » are specifically responsible for the active management of those risks that can affect the outcome of the project or program; and

» ensure that any project or program risks that could have a significant business impact are raised with either the chief risk officer or chief financial officer.

» Business unit managers/directors:
  » are responsible for the management of risks within their business unit; and
  » ensure any risks that have wider business impact are raised with the chief risk officer or chief financial officer.

With an increasing focus on shareholder value and value-based reporting, the responsibilities for risk reporting have grown considerably. Whereas financial institutions have to report on market, credit, and operational risk, organizations (whose core business is not finance) have to take a much broader stance. The way to achieve this is to ensure that the responsibility for identifying and managing risks is carefully defined throughout the organization. This also helps to establish a culture that accepts risk as part of its daily activities rather than treat it as taboo (see Chapter 10 and the 10 steps to success). In organizations that take risk management seriously, these roles and responsibilities are typically augmented by risk management committees focused on specific risk categories. For example, the use of project and program boards focus on the management of the major risks that affect the project or program; operational risk management committees focus on the wide-ranging risks that affect the operational viability of the organization, and credit risk committees focus on the risks of loan defaults and so on.

A LOOK TO THE FUTURE

The factors that have made risk management an important skill within the modern corporation are unlikely to diminish. If anything, technological change, globalization, activism, online fraud, and hacking will increase. Therefore the need for everyone in the organization to understand the process of risk management will become ever more important. Responding to the risks that organizations face will lead to many appointing chief risk officers, whose role will be to

THE STATE OF THE ART 59

manage enterprise-wide risks and ensure risk is appropriately managed throughout the organization. Some have already done so.

KEY LEARNING POINTS
State of the art

1 Managing the risks of globalization requires organizations to:
   » think about the issues;
   » identify the stakeholders and develop close working relationships with them;
   » think in scenarios;
   » build and integrate new competencies; and
   » engage nongovernmental organizations.
2 Managing technical risks involves the following strategies:
   » obtaining more cash at a given point in time;
   » reducing cash inflows;
   » obtaining the same cash outflows but at a later stage;
   » reducing the risks of cash outflows; and
   » adopting a trickle-up rather than trickle-down approach to market risk.
3 Operational risk management requires organizations to establish a risk management framework that includes:
   » strategy;
   » policies;
   » risk management processes;
   » risk mitigation strategies;
   » operations management; and
   » culture.
4 The risks associated with the electronic channel can be managed by:
   » establishing a transparent policy for e-mail;
   » managing the product development process by using a flexible approach to project management;
   » fully understanding the risk factors associated with online fraud; and
   » guarding against the risks of unauthorized access.

5 Organizations must establish appropriate responsibility for the management of risk at all levels.

6 Organizations will increasingly appoint chief risk officers.

NOTES

1 Quoted in Ledger, W. (2001) "Keeping out of cyber strife." *Evening Standard*, July 16, p. 44.

2 Steinberg, R. and Bromilow, C. (2000) *Corporate Governance and the Board – What Works Best*. The Institute of Internal Auditors Research Foundation, Florida, p. 17.

In Practice: Risk Management Success Stories

Managing risk is not simple, but many organizations have learnt to manage the risks they face. This chapter includes the following case studies:

» Shell;
» Xerox;
» Mattel;
» a global bank;
» Nike;
» project success; and
» a UK utility.

"Take calculated risks. That is quite different from being rash."
General George S Patton, US General
"What is clear at a boardroom level is that strong risk management
is an essential part of good corporate governance and something
that helps to protect shareholder value."
Chris Frost, Dave Allen, James Porter, and Phillip Bloodworth,
risk management consultants

SHELL – MANAGING STRATEGIC RISK THROUGH SCENARIO PLANNING[1]

Shell first became interested in scenarios in the late 1960s when the
existing planning process, based upon forecasting, repeatedly failed.
Scenarios were introduced as a way of avoiding having to predict
the unpredictable. This was not as simple as it sounds because, in
order to develop scenarios, Shell had to gather and analyze large
volumes of data about the various drivers and factors that built up
each scenario. One of the earliest factors that Shell considered was
the price of oil. At that time, during the late 1960s, the outlook for
demand was very predictable, growing at 6% per year. Equally, supply
was believed to be plentiful, and as demand rose, all that was required
were a few more wells. But one key concern remained the control
of the oil reserves. This was important because the governments of
the oil-producing nations of the Middle East were beginning to exert
their power over the oil companies. And it was believed by Shell that
the demands of the oil companies might not always be met in the
future.

This uncertainty formed the basis of six scenarios, one of which
was named the *crisis scenario*. This thinking was to prove beneficial
during the oil crisis of 1973, although not for all operating divisions. The Manufacturing Division (which converted crude oil into its
constituent products) took the scenarios seriously and planned their
operations with them in mind. When the oil crisis struck, they were
ready and took appropriate action. In contrast, the Marine Division
(which was responsible for transporting oil overseas) felt scenarios
were not relevant to their business. They believed that, even if a
crisis occurred, people would still require oil. And although they
were shocked when the crisis hit, they did not take significant action

because they believed it was only a temporary phenomenon. By the time they reacted, a massive over-capacity in the world's oil transportation fleet had developed that destroyed Marine's profitability for years.

In general, however, Shell was able to manage the risks of the oil crisis very well, because it recognized the beginnings of the *crisis scenario* when prices started to rise in 1973. Whilst the rest of the oil refining industry spent years deciding what to do, Shell moved rapidly by switching investments from expansion of primary capacity to upgrading the output of the refineries to focus on high value products such as gasoline. As a result, Shell outperformed the rest of the industry for most of the 1970s and early 1980s.

Shell followed this success by renewing its approach to environmental issues, which once again was based upon scenario planning. The scenario in this case, which was developed in 1989, described a world in which the environment was a major issue and only those organizations that took the environment seriously would survive. This approach ensured that any new project was carefully assessed for environmental consequences before it was started.

According to Kees van der Heijden, author of *Scenarios: The Art of Strategic Conversation*, Shell benefited from scenarios in five ways.

» They found that their strategic decisions and project investments were more robust under different potential futures, thereby future-proofing them.
» They became much better at thinking about the future.
» They enabled their manufacturing personnel to become more perceptive and begin to recognize events as being part of a pattern, rather than isolated incidents.
» They were able to set a wider context for decision-making down the line instead of dictating precise and direct instructions.
» They were able to use scenarios as a leadership tool.

After more than 25 years of scenario planning, Shell would not manage their strategic risks any other way.

XEROX – MANAGING TECHNICAL AND MARKET RISKS[2]

Xerox is a multinational corporation specializing in document management and production equipment plus associated technologies. Its annual revenues in 2000 were in the region of $19bn. This revenue was augmented by a further $7bn from Fuji Xerox, the photographic company.

The challenge for organizations such as Xerox is to grow revenues whilst at the same time having a steady stream of new products entering the market. This is especially important because they operate within the highly innovative and fast-moving technology sector. Because of speed and competition, product and market risks loom large. To accomplish its growth and innovation goals, Xerox spends 6% of its revenue on research, development, and engineering, of which 80% goes on product engineering and manufacturing and 20% on advanced research and technology development. More importantly, this investment is managed rigorously through a disciplined innovation and product delivery process which drives down both the risks of product failure but, more importantly, market failure. This process consists of the seven steps below and is fed by an ongoing research program that generates new product ideas and market innovations:

1 pre-concept
2 concept
3 design
4 demonstration
5 production
6 launch
7 maintenance.

The process is front-loaded with a technology development mechanism that takes the research ideas and assesses their performance potential along with their robustness and any manufacturing issues. This is the principal way Xerox manages its product risk. The second purpose is to refine the product requirements, thereby reducing the level of market risk. At any one time something in the region of 300 projects are passing through the process, of which around 90 are launched annually.

Xerox is careful to match its products to both the market and its own strategic direction. In particular, because the market risks are directly related to customer requirements and expectations, Xerox continuously tests the viability of the product against a number of factors including customer and user needs, market functions and capabilities, emerging technologies, other technology options, and technology functions and capabilities. In the past, Xerox have got it wrong, as the following examples illustrate. However, they have been able to learn from the experience and that is essential in the management of risk.

» In 1981 they launched the Xerox 6085 professional workstation with ViewPoint icons and windowing software. This was a new product in an untried market, so there was no direct competition. With the best scientists working on the product development, the product was technically sound. Unfortunately, the customer requirements were not well known, so market risk was higher than it ought to have been. In the end, the only big user of the 6085 personal workstation was Xerox itself. Commercially, the product failed and production eventually ceased.

» Liveboard, a computationally active whiteboard with remote communications ability, was launched without fully understanding the market risk. Xerox believed that the market had to be there and so did not follow a rigorous assessment of the market prior to launch. Because the product depended on Unix, many organizations found it incompatible with their Microsoft-based desktop and office automation systems. Xerox substituted Microsoft Windows for Unix but lost many of the product advantages in the process. In the end, the product was withdrawn.

When assessing product and market risk, Xerox uses six factors. In terms of product risk, it assesses the risk of not being able to resolve any remaining technical problems prior to launch, the risk of not having the competencies and complementary technologies available to commercialize the product, and the risk of the technical specification failing to meet customer expectations. In terms of market risk, it assesses the risk of not being able to deliver the product, the risk of the product not providing sufficient differentiation in the market, and the risk of the product not selling. Each of these is assessed throughout the product development process and simple algorithms and tools are used to assess the severity of the risks (from very high through low). In this way, Xerox are able to make good use of their investment funds and reduce the risks of product and market failure by pulling the plug on the development if either the product or market risks become too high.

MATTEL – MANAGING BRAND RISK[3]

As part of its review of its most profitable products, Mattel took a long hard look at its Barbie doll. In its analysis it realized that, despite its popularity with young girls, it caused some problems with their parents who were concerned with the image that it portrayed, especially in relation to the stereotypical view of the way women should look. It also discovered that many of its female employees were embarrassed to tell friends and acquaintances that they were associated with the product. Mattel recognized that this could, over time, not only affect the success of its best-selling product, but also the brand position of Mattel itself, which sold many other products. Ultimately this would affect market position and revenue for the firm. It perceived a future in which Barbie was seen to be uncool by parents and children alike. In response, it repositioned Barbie to reflect a more positive image of women, thereby protecting both the revenue streams from the doll, and more importantly the brand image of Mattel as a whole.

A GLOBAL BANK – ENHANCING THE PROCESS OF MANAGING ITS FINANCIAL RISK

Following losses arising from the failure of the Long-Term Capital Management hedge fund in the third quarter of 1998, the bank reviewed and revised its risk management framework. In late 1998, the board of directors endorsed the findings of the review and agreed that attention be paid to:

» incorporating operational risks within the risk management and control processes of the bank;
» reinforcing efforts to ensure the completeness and accuracy of data that supports the risk management decision-making process;
» ensuring that assessments of risk/return potential of particular business activities take into account risk considerations;

» ensuring there is a structured process in place throughout the group to assess risks in new business ventures; and

» reorienting the bank's approach to measuring and limiting risk exposures towards potential loss in extreme market conditions as well as normal conditions.

The bank also updated its risk policy framework, which sets the overall guidelines for risk management and control at the bank. The framework distinguishes between three functions within the process. These are *risk management*, which is defined as managing the bank's exposure to risk within the overall guidelines and limits approved by the board of directors (adherence to the policy and the limits set out within it is the responsibility of the management of the business divisions and individual business lines); *logistics*, which includes financial control, operations, and information technology, and performs an essential control function when processing the transactions of the bank; and *risk control*, which covers the independent risk control functions that report to the chief risk officer and chief credit officer of the bank.

The bank manages its risks in the following ways.

» By having an effective process for managing and controlling risk, which itself depends upon the ability to identify the risks the bank faces and establishing a comprehensive set of limits and procedures to control them once identified.

» By ensuring the bank's appetite for risk and its risk-bearing capability are reflected in its limits and procedures. The board of directors sets the risk limits by assessing the group's risk appetite and risk-bearing capacity. The former is a measure of the risk which the board of directors believes the group requires to deliver satisfactory long-term growth and return on equity (represented by Value at Risk). The board of directors also sets limits on the potential stress loss the bank could face in extreme market conditions (such as those experienced at the time of the failure of the Long-Term Capital Management hedge fund) based on its risk-bearing capacity. This capacity takes into account the bank's overall earnings capacity, and is set to protect the group from unacceptable damage to annual earnings, dividend-paying ability, business viability, and reputation.

Risk appetite and risk-bearing capacity are reviewed regularly to take into account any changes in the market.

» By ensuring there is an appropriate management structure through which the risk management and control process operates. The group executive board is responsible for setting the bank's overall risk management framework. In establishing the framework, the group allocates risk limits to the divisions and monitors the risk profile at group level. Within the group executive board, the chief risk officer and chief credit officer are responsible for ensuring there are consistent policies and procedures across the group for measuring, managing, and reporting on risk. The market and credit risk control functions are independent from the business and are staffed by experienced employees located in the respective business divisions. Each division also has risk management committees, which involve senior business managers together with representatives of the risk control functions. The committee ensures that there is an ongoing review of the risk profile of the division in respect of all the material risks it faces. Finally, group internal audit reviews and evaluates the effectiveness of the risk policy framework and associated control frameworks.

» By assessing management's ability to manage and control risks in an effective manner.

» By ensuring it has the internal capabilities, such as information technology, and suitably qualified staff.

» By having an excellent understanding of the external environment.

NIKE – RESPONDING TO THE RISKS OF GLOBALIZATION[4]

As we saw in Chapter 5, globalization has increased the need for effective corporate and social responsibility. Back in 1994, the annual salary of Nike's chief executive officer, Phil Knight, was $1.5mn, which was 1500 times more than its workers in China received. At that time it would have taken 15 centuries for them to earn the same. This disparity came to a head when a number of nongovernmental organizations demonstrated during the opening of Nike's shop in San Francisco. The issue concerned the amounts paid to front line workers (approximately $1.44 per pair) when compared to how much the shoes were actually sold for (approximately $80 per pair). But it also went far beyond just wages and the marking up of products. Issues such as Nike repeatedly shifting production to regions with the cheapest labor costs added to the growing belief that Nike was a poor corporate citizen.

At the time, Nike responded by stating that the workers should believe themselves to be fortunate enough to have a job and that the issues of how much people were paid should be put before the United Nations, rather than Nike. But in 1998, Phil Knight responded to the criticisms more positively, initially acknowledging the underestimating of public concern over the issue of worker exploitation. This was followed by a series of new policies designed to improve working conditions through the elimination of hazardous chemicals in the production process, researching into international manufacturing processes, and starting a program that independently checked the working conditions of the manufacturing plants.

THE STANDISH STUDY – SUCCESSFUL PROJECTS[5]

During the 1990s, the Standish Group, a US-based market and technology research firm, investigated the factors that led to IT project failure. As well assessing projects that had failed, they also tried to understand what caused projects to succeed. The research identified the following 10 factors:

» user involvement
» executive management support
» clear statements of requirements
» proper planning
» realistic expectations
» smaller project milestones
» competent staff
» ownership
» clear vision and objectives
» hard-working and focused staff.

Organizations would be wise to take the Standish Group's advice, especially as the failure of IT projects in the US alone is believed to be in the region of 35% and costs business some $81bn annually. Consider the following two cases that contrast the financial impact of successful and unsuccessful risk management strategies in projects.

Hyatt Hotels successfully developed a reservation system that allowed people to dial from an airplane at 35,000 feet, check into their hotel, schedule a courtesy bus to pick them up from the airport, and have their hotel keys ready at the reservation desk. This system cost $15mn to develop.

Contrast this with the CONFIRM project, which was a combined travel reservation system. In 1988 a consortium comprising Hilton National Hotels, Marriott, and Budget Rent-A-Car subcontracted a large-scale project to AMR information services, a subsidiary of American Airlines. In this project they were to develop a leading edge, comprehensive travel industry reservation system. But the system was never fully built and, after experiencing substantial problems in testing, it was abandoned after three-and-a-half years at a cost of $125mn.[6]

A UK UTILITY – MANAGING MULTIPLE RISKS AT A TIME OF GREAT CHANGE

As part of the deregulation of the UK's gas market, this organization faced massive changes in the way it operated and dealt with its customers. In addition, it faced intense scrutiny from the regulator, who wanted to see its monopoly within the market broken up. This would mean that individual customers, some 19 million in total, would have the option to switch their gas supplier. The utility had no option but to respond to the demands of the regulator, and this meant establishing a change program that would touch every part of the organization. The principal risks it faced were:

» regulatory risks associated with the timescales set for the introduction of domestic competition and the implications of failing to comply;
» technical risks associated with the need to overhaul major parts of its IT infrastructure and systems which accompanied the change;
» operational risks that would impact business-as-usual operations, as well as the need to cope with the anticipated level of queries from customers as they switched suppliers;

» financial risks associated with resolving outstanding invoices and dealing with the queries associated with apportioning revenue between the various suppliers; and

» program and project risks in terms of how failure could impact the successful outcome the utility was seeking.

The utility responded by establishing a series of programs focused on the key elements of the change. These programs included an IT program charged with the introduction of the new IT systems and infrastructure, an invoicing program to manage the clean-up of old invoicing records and queries, an organizational change program that would create the new operational environment and working practices, and a program that would develop the new legal framework in which gas supply would be managed.

Managing the regulatory risks involved two aspects. First, the ongoing dialog with the regulator and the new gas suppliers. This was not only crucial during the legal changes that had to be made, but also essential in establishing a foundation of trust once domestic competition had been introduced. The second element involved keeping the regulator abreast of progress toward domestic competition but, more importantly, of the risks. Engaging the regulator early within the risk management process ensured a realistic dialog about deadlines and allowed the right decisions to be made about the implementation schedule.

Because of the nature of the technical task, technical risk had to be managed very carefully. The utility was in uncharted territory with respect to what they wanted to achieve with the way customer records were to be managed. The likelihood of hardware and software failure was very real. The risks were managed by:

» establishing close working relationships with the hardware vendors;

» bringing expert technical expertise to help in the construction of the new system;

» adopting an incremental implementation strategy; and

» freezing any other system changes apart from those associated with preparing the organization for Year 2000.

Operational risks were principally dealt with by employing large numbers of temporary staff to manage the administrative overhead created by the changes (particularly those associated with closing out old accounts and dealing with the paperwork when customers changed from one supplier to another). In addition, models of the likely level of queries the organization would receive once domestic competition was introduced were used to develop contingency plans for bringing in additional temporary staff to work around the clock to resolve them.

In order to manage the financial risks associated with how much money was owed either to the utility or to other shippers, a complex approach was adopted to ensure objectivity and an acceptable outcome. Success was not just based upon a formulaic process, as face-to-face negotiations were necessary to ensure the outcome was satisfactory to both the shipper community and the utility. Had it been badly managed, the utility may have had to bear significant costs.

In order to manage the program and project level risks, program and project offices were established for each of the major streams of work. In addition, an overview program was established that tied all of the programs together to provide a strategic level view of progress and risks. This information was fed directly into the board on a bi-weekly basis.

Domestic competition was successfully introduced and was hailed as a huge success by the regulator and the gas industry as a whole. But it was only through the effective management of risk at all levels that such a result was possible.

KEY INSIGHTS

A number of conclusions can be drawn from the collective analysis of the case studies.

1 Managing risk takes a degree of courage.
2 Managing risk requires action, not rhetoric. It also requires open and honest dialogue.
3 It is important to learn from errors of judgment and past mistakes.

4 Sometimes it is necessary to embrace your enemies (NGOs, competitors, and regulators) in order to manage risk.

5 Managing risk requires the organization to take responsibility for its actions and not blame others for the problems and issues it faces.

NOTES

1 For an in-depth analysis of the Shell experience see van der Heijden, K. (1996) *Scenarios: The Art of Strategic Conversation.* John Wiley & Sons, New York, pp. 15–22.

2 See Branscomb, L. and Auerswald, P. (2001) *Taking Technical Risks.* The MIT Press, Cambridge, MA.

3 Schwartz, P. and Gibb, B. (1999) *When Good Companies Do Bad Things: Responsibility and Risk in an Age of Globalization.* John Wiley & Sons, New York, p. 69.

4 This case study is based upon a discussion on Nike and its approach to corporate and sociability in Schwartz, P. and Gibb, B. (1999) *When Good Companies Do Bad Things: Responsibility and Risk in an Age of Globalization.* John Wiley & Sons, New York, pp. 51–5.

5 Gallagher, K. (1995) "Chaos." Conference Proceedings, Information Technology and Project Management, September 19–20 1995, pp. 21–36.

6 Oz, E. (1994) "When professional standards are lax: The CONFIRM failure and its lessons." *Communications of the ACM*, Vol. 37, No. 10.

Key Concepts and Thinkers

Risk management has many terms and concepts. This chapter covers the majority of them.

What follows is a glossary containing the key terms associated with risk and risk management, as well as some more general terms associated with the subject of finance.

ACID – This acronym refers to electronic transactions, which if they are to be trusted should be:

» **A**tomic – the transaction cannot be split into its component parts and will either fail completely or succeed completely;

» **C**onsistent – a transaction is said to be consistent if all parties involved agree on the critical facts of the exchange;

» **I**solated – transactions do not interfere with each other; and

» **D**urable – when a failure occurs, the transaction can be recovered to its last consistent state.

ACID transactions are robust because they are unaffected by failures of any kind (human, network, and hardware).

Accounting policies – Those principles and practices applied by an entity that specify how the effects of transactions and other events are to be reflected in the accounts. For example, an entity may have a policy of revaluing fixed assets or of maintaining them at historical cost. Accounting policies do not include estimation techniques.

Accounts payable – American terminology for creditors.

Accounts receivable – American terminology for debtors.

Accrual – An expense or a proportion thereof not invoiced prior to the balance sheet date but included in the accounts sometimes on an estimated basis.

Accruals concept – Income and expenses are recognized in the period in which they are earned or incurred, rather than the period in which they happen to be received or paid.

Asset – Any property or rights owned by the company that have a monetary value. In UK accounting standards, assets are defined as "rights or other access to future economic benefits controlled by an entity as a result of past transactions or events."

Balance sheet – A statement describing what a business owns and owes at a particular date.

Basle Accord – The 1988 Basle Accord (also known as the Bank for International Standards Accord) was designed to establish a set of international guidelines that linked a bank's credit exposure to its minimum capital requirement. Although initially focused on credit risk, subsequent amendments have extended this to market risk and risk-based capital requirements.

Break-even point – The level of activity at which the fixed costs of a project are just covered by the contribution from sales. At this point there is neither a profit nor a loss.

Break-even analysis – A form of analysis that relates activity to totals of revenue and costs based on the classification of costs into fixed and variable.

Business continuity planning – Interest in business continuity planning has grown considerably since the corporate world was shocked into preparing for the worst with the Year 2000 date change. Although Year 2000 came and went without any great disasters, the heightened awareness of business continuity planning remained. Although business continuity planning is often assumed to be about maintaining business operations following a natural disaster such as an earthquake, the majority of disasters are caused by power outages and fire. According to James Barnes, author of *A Guide to Business Continuity Planning*, there are at least 75 known causes for a disaster condition ranging from the very serious, such as volcanoes and hurricanes, to the minor, such as insect infestation.

The process of creating business continuity plans usually follows five steps.[1]

1 Establishing the project that develops the business continuity plan. This involves the standard project management activities associated with setting up any project.

2 Assessing the internal and external threats to the business. This involves assessing the criticality of business processes and systems along with their resource requirements and determining the recovery time for each.

3 Selecting an appropriate strategy to enhance the survivability of the critical components of the business. This is really about managing the risk by reducing their likelihood or impact.

4 Developing the business continuity plan. The purpose of the plan is to recreate the critical business components should they fail. This is all about re-establishing normal business activity as soon as possible after a disaster strikes.

5 Testing and maintaining the plan once developed.

Capital Asset Pricing Model (CAPM) – A theoretical framework comparing risk and return on shares. According to the model, financial markets will compensate investors for taking market risk, but not on specific risk (which can be diversified away).

Capital employed – The aggregate amount of long-term funds invested in or lent to the business and used by it in carrying out its operations.

Cashflow forecast – A statement of future, anticipated cash balances based on estimated cash inflows and outflows over a given period.

Cashflow statement – A statement of cashflows during the most recent accounting period. The required format for a cashflow statement is laid down in accounting standards.

Collateralized Debt Obligations (CDO) – Securities backed by pools of bonds or loans. Their purpose is to reduce an investor's exposure to an individual bond or loan by pooling a variety of credits, typically junk bonds, and using the cashflow to back securities with different risk ratings.

Comparability – The requirement that once an accounting policy for a particular item in the accounts has been adopted, the same policy should be used from one period to the next. Any change in policy must be fully disclosed. Comparability is also important when comparing entities in the same industry. They should, wherever possible, use similar accounting policies.

Contingent liability – A possible obligation arising from past events whose existence will be confirmed only by the occurrence of one or more uncertain future events not wholly within the entity's control.

Costs of capital – The weighted average costs of funds to a company based on the mix of equity and loan capital and their respective costs. This is sometimes used as the required rate of return in a discounted cashflow.

Costs of goods sold (or Cost of sales) – Those costs (usually raw materials, labor, and production overheads) directly attributable to goods that have been sold. The difference between sales and cost of goods sold is gross profit.

Country risk – Country risk is the risk that a counterparty will not be able to pay its obligations because of cross-border restrictions on the availability of a given currency. Where the country's economy is weak, or their political situation poor, their risk rating tends to be high.

Credit rating - Every company issuing debt is rated according to its creditworthiness by two major agencies, Standard & Poor's and Moody's. The rating is based upon a combination of the default risk and the likelihood of payment for the issuer.

  » For those organizations that are believed to be capable of meeting their financial obligations, their credit ratings range from AAA through AA to A. This means that the organization concerned has a low credit risk.

  » For those organizations that are more vulnerable to changes in economic or market conditions and are therefore more likely to find it difficult (or are unwilling) to meet their financial obligations, their credit ratings range from BBB+/BBB through BBB−, and BB+/BB to BB− (the plus and minus signs indicate the relative position within the ratings, and are important differentiators).

  » For those organizations that are the most vulnerable to non-payment and are particularly exposed to adverse economic and market conditions, their rating ranges from CCC through CC to C. Such organizations have the highest credit risk.

  Those organizations with a rating of AAA, AA, A, and BBB are considered to be of investment grade. Those rated lower are not investment grade and are considered to be more risky and speculative.

Credit risk - The risk associated with the ability (or willingness) of a third party to repay money owed. The creditworthiness of an organization determines the interest rate paid on the loan and the amount of collateral required to secure the loan in the first place.

Creditors - Amounts due to those who have supplied goods or services to the business.

Currency exchange risk - The risk associated with the value of foreign currency holdings caused by fluctuations in the currency markets.

Current asset - An asset which, if not already in cash form, is expected to be converted into cash within 12 months of the balance sheet date.

Current cost – The convention by which assets are valued at the cost of replacement at the balance sheet date (net of depreciation for fixed assets).

Current liability – An amount owed which will have to be paid within 12 months of the balance sheet date.

Current ratio – The ratio of current assets to current liabilities in a balance sheet, providing a measure of business liquidity.

Debentures – Long-term loans, usually secured on the company's assets.

Debtors – Amounts due from customers to whom goods or services have been sold but for which they have not yet paid.

Deferred asset/liability – An amount receivable or payable more than 12 months after the balance sheet date.

Deferred taxation – An estimate of a tax liability payable at some estimated future date, resulting from timing differences in the taxation and accounting treatment of certain items of income and expenditure.

Delphi process – The Delphi process is a forecasting technique that is based upon the repetitive polling of experts. The process involves seeking the opinion of a group of experts on a particular subject, such as the closing value of the Dow Jones index on December 31. Once the experts have made their forecast the results are shared anonymously across the group. Each can then modify his or her forecast in light of the group results. The process continues until the results stabilize.

Depreciation – An estimate of the proportion of the cost of a fixed asset which has been consumed (whether through use, obsolescence, or the passage of time) during the accounting period.

Derivatives – A derivative is a financial instrument that derives its value from the value of other instruments.

Discounted cashflow (DCF) – A method of appraisal for investment projects. The total incremental stream of cash for a project is tested to assess the level of return it delivers to the investor. If the return exceeds the required, or hurdle, rate the project is recommended on financial terms or vice versa.

Distribution – The amount distributed to shareholders out of the profits of the company, usually in the form of a cash dividend.

Diversification – A risk management strategy which involves investing in different market sectors and countries as a means of reducing exposure to market risk.

Dividend cover – The ratio of the amount of profit reported for the year to the amount distributed.

Dividend yield – The ratio of the amount of dividend per share to the market share price of a listed company.

Earnings per share – The amount of profit (after tax and any extraordinary items) attributable to shareholders divided by the number of ordinary shares in issue.

EBIT – Earnings (profit) before interest and tax.

EBITDA – Earnings (profit) before interest, tax, depreciation, and amortization. This measure of operating cashflow is considered to be an important measure of the performance of an entity.

Estimation techniques – The methods adopted by an entity to arrive at estimated monetary amounts for items in the accounts. For example, of the various methods that could be adopted for depreciation, the entity may select to depreciate using the straight-line method.

Exceptional item – Income or expenditure that, although arising from the ordinary course of business, is of such unusual size or incidence that it needs to be disclosed separately.

Expense – A cost incurred, or a proportion of a cost, the benefit of which is wholly used up in the earning of the revenue for a particular accounting period.

Extraordinary item – Material income or expenditure arising from outside the ordinary course of business. As a result of recent changes to accounting standards, it is considered that extraordinary items are extremely rare if not non-existent.

Fixed asset – Asset held for use by the business rather than for sale.

Fixed cost – A cost that does not vary in proportion to changes in the scale of operations, e.g. rent.

Fraud detection technologies[2] – Online merchants have a number of fraud detection technologies available to them with which to manage the risks of online theft. If used in combination, they can be quite effective.

» *Address verification systems*. These validate the billing address provided by the purchaser against the billing address information held by the card issuer.

» *Card verification methods*. This consists of a 3–4 digit code that is printed but not embossed on the card, or contained within the magnetic strip. The online merchant can request the number as an additional security measure. Should the card be counterfeit, it will not contain this number.

» *Lockout mechanisms*. These are specifically designed to prevent randomly generated credit card numbers from being used by fraudsters. The usual traits of a randomly generated card attack include multiple transactions with similar card numbers, a large number of declined transactions, and the failure of the address verification test.

» *Negative lists*. These hold information that can be used by the online merchant to assess the level of risk a transaction might represent. For example, the lists hold information about charge-backs against particular card numbers, odd billing addresses, and known countries where fraud is rife, such as Nigeria and Eastern Europe.

» *Fraud rules*. These are designed to pinpoint high risk transactions using a rules-based selection process. The rules can vary and are often designed by the online merchant. Examples include purchases over a certain amount, multiple purchases of a single item, and so on.

» *Risk scoring*. These are tools based on statistical models of fraudulent transactions and are probably the most effective detection mechanisms available to online merchants.

Gearing – Gearing is the word used to describe the financing of the company in terms of the proportion of capital provided by shareholders (equity) compared with the proportion provided by loan capital (debt).

Gearing ratios – There are many different ways to measure gearing. The commonest is probably the ratio of debt to equity. That is the ratio of long-term loans to shareholders' funds (which can be measured in terms of nominal value or market value). Another common approach (called the capital gearing ratio) is to calculate the percentage of debt to total capital (debt plus equity). The income gearing ratio is the ratio of interest payable to the profits out of which interest is paid.

Gross profit - The difference between sales and the cost of goods sold.

Hedging - Hedging is a way of dealing with unwanted risks. Hedging involves acquiring a new risk that completely offsets the unwanted risk. The net effect of this is zero, resulting in no loss or gain. However, it is rare to find a completely safe hedge, as they usually cost something, and in some cases they can go disastrously wrong, as with Long-Term Capital Management in 1998. The primary financial instruments for hedging are:

» *Forwards*. An agreement to buy or sell shares in a company, foreign exchange, or a commodity at an agreed rate at a specified point in the future. The buyer in the deal is said to be taking the long position and the seller the short position. The specified point in the future when the deal is executed is the maturity date and the agreed price is the delivery price.

» *Swaps*. An agreement between two parties to exchange each other's commitments at an agreed rate at a specified point in the future. Swaps are usually associated with interest rates and currencies. Swaps have been around since the 1920s but have only been popular within the financial markets since the 1980s. Interest rate swaps are where two parties agree to meet each other's interest rate payments when they become due. Currency swaps are more complex because it can be difficult to cover the risk entirely owing to the variations in currencies. As a result it is usual for a swap to consist of two or more agreements.

» *Options*. These give someone the right (not the obligation) to buy or sell shares, currency, and commodities at an agreed price at a specified point in the future. The key distinction here is that, unlike swaps and forwards, the buyer does not have to purchase should market conditions be more favorable. The price at which the shares, currency, or commodities can be purchased is known as the exercise price, and taking up the right is known as exercising. The date at which the option is (or not) exercised is called the expiration date.

Historic cost convention – The convention by which assets are valued on the basis of the original cost of acquiring or producing them.

Hurdle rate – The rate of return decided on by a company as the minimum acceptable for capital investment. It will be governed by the company's cost of capital and it may allow for different levels of risk.

Interest cover – The relationship between the amount of profit (before interest and before tax) and the amount of interest payable during a period.

Interest rate risk – The risk associated with the value of fixed income obligations changing as a result of more favorable terms being available on the open market.

Internal rate of return (IRR) – The rate of discount that brings the present value of all the cashflows associated with a capital investment to zero. It measures the effective yield on the investment. If this yield is greater than the hurdle rate the investment is seen to be financially desirable and vice versa.

Liability – An amount owed. In UK accounting standards, liabilities are defined as "an entity's obligations to transfer economic benefits as a result of past transactions or events."

Liquidity – A term used to describe the cash resources of a business and its ability to meet its short-term obligations.

Liquidity risk – Probably the most important and least understood risk. It relates to the ability (or inability) to buy or sell something at short notice at a fair or good rate. Liquidity risk is usually the result of buyers not being found fast enough. From a purely market perspective, liquidity risk occurs when markets do not perform in a perfect way. When there is a danger of a global lack of liquidity, such as with the Year 2000, central banks can take deliberate steps to ensure markets remain liquid in times of crisis.

Listed investments – Investments the market price for which is quoted on a recognized stock exchange. They may therefore be traded on that exchange.

Long-term liability - An amount payable more than 12 months after the balance sheet date.

Market price - The price of a quoted security for dealing in the open market.

Monte Carlo simulation - Named after the roulette wheels in Monte Carlo, which are considered to be mechanisms for generating random numbers. Creating a Monte Carlo simulation involves four steps.

1   To begin with, it is necessary to develop a cashflow model for the investment or business model under analysis. This involves capturing information about inputs such as costs (fixed and variable), sales, interest rates and prices and outputs such as revenues, annual cash-flows, and rates of return. The cashflow model is usually built in a spreadsheet for ease of use.

2   Having identified the inputs and outputs, it is necessary to model the uncertainties of the key inputs using a probability distribution based upon historic data, expert opinion, scenario analysis, or management opinion. This essentially shows how the value of the input variable changes across the distribution, be it normal, skewed normal, and so on.

3   Next, it is necessary to identify the relationships between the input variables. With the operating environments of most businesses being highly complex, it is rare to find that the variables are independent of each other.

4   Finally, the simulation is run. This involves selecting samples of the input variables across the probability distributions, calculating the outputs, and presenting these as a probability distribution.

Net assets - The amount of total assets less total liabilities.

Net book value - The cost (or valuation) of fixed assets less accumulated depreciation to date. Net book value bears no relationship to market value.

Net current assets - The amount of current assets less current liabilities.

Net present value (NPV) - A positive or negative value arrived at by discounting the cashflow from a capital project by the desired rate of return. If the value is positive, it means that the project is desirable and vice versa.

Net realizable value – Amount at which an asset could be sold in its existing condition at the balance sheet date, after deducting any costs to be incurred in disposing of it.

Nominal value – The face value of a share or other security.

Operational risk – Risks caused by losses associated with mistakes, failure of information systems, deliberate sabotage by staff, poor internal controls, and disasters (such as flooding, hurricanes, and so on). Operational risks are more vague than the other forms of risk and require more effort to define them. However, failure to manage them can lead to significant financial loss.

Opportunity cost – The alternative advantage foregone as a result of the commitment of resources to one particular end.

Overhead – Any expense, other than the direct cost of materials or labor, involved in making a company's products.

Payback period – A term used in investment appraisal. It refers to the time required for the non-discounted cash inflow to accumulate to the initial cash outflow in the investment.

Prepayment – The part of a cost which is carried forward as an asset in the balance sheet to be recognized as an expense in the ensuing period(s) in which the benefit will be derived from it, e.g. the payment in advance of rates.

Price/earnings ratio – The relationship between the market price of a share and its latest reported earnings per share.

Profit – The difference between the revenues earned in the period and the costs incurred in earning them. Alternative definitions are possible according to whether the figure is struck before or after tax.

Profit and loss account – A statement summarizing the revenues and the costs incurred in earning them during an accounting period.

Program and project risk – The risk associated with the failure of a major project or program. Because most change in organizations is now stepwise rather than incremental, the importance of programs and projects has increased significantly, as have the risks associated with their failure.

Provision – A liability of uncertain timing or amount. A provision should only be recognized in the balance sheet when an entity has a present obligation (legal or constructive) as a result of a past event, it is probable that a transfer of economic benefits will be required to settle the obligation, and a reliable estimate can be made of the amount of the obligation. Unless these conditions are met, no provision should be recognized.

Quick ratio - The ratio of those current assets readily convertible into cash (usually current assets less stock) to current liabilities.

Residual value - A notional cash inflow attributed to a capital project to allow for value remaining in the project at the final year of the assessment.

Revaluation reserve - The increase in value of a fixed asset as a result of a revaluation. This needs to be included in the balance sheet as part of shareholders' funds in order to make the balance sheet balance.

Revenue reserves - The accumulated amount of profit less losses generated by the company since its incorporation and retained in it. It is usually called "profit and loss account" in the balance sheet.

Revenue - Money received from selling the product of the business.

Risk culture - According to John Holiwell,[3] the risk culture in an organization is a critical factor in the management of risk. Creating an appropriate risk culture means three things.

1 Understanding the board's appetite for risk. This is important, as it dictates how much risk the organization is prepared to take.

2 Being honest. There is little point in taking risks if the consequences of them are hidden from view or if, when they are raised, they are ignored. Being honest means having open discussions and being willing to take the necessary actions to manage risk.

3 Ensuring risk management is understood throughout the organization.

Risk management general process - The process through which risks are identified, managed, and controlled. Risk management involves a continuous process that has four basic steps.

1 *Identification*. The process of identifying risks will vary according to its nature. Whereas most financial risks are identified using sophisticated models, operational and project risks require more qualitative approaches, such as structured thinking, brainstorming, scenario analysis, and so on.

2 *Quantification*. The process of quantification involves evaluating each risk (or a collection of risks, where they interact) to determine

the impact and the likelihood of their materializing. Again, there are various tools to help, such as simulations, decision tree analysis, use of experts, and so on.

3 *Response development.* Although every identified risk needs a response, those that have only a limited impact may be allowed to follow their course because the costs of avoiding them may outweigh their impacts. When developing a response, a number of options are open to the risk manager. Risks can be avoided by taking actions to ensure they pose no threat at all, although this may mean taking an entirely different path in the investment, business or program/project. If they can't be avoided, action can be taken to reduce either the impact or likelihood. And if all else fails, some form of contingency plan can be developed that allows the risk to be dealt with once it has materialized. The risks posed by the Year 2000 date change were managed through a combination of reduction and avoidance strategies. This involved retiring old hardware, changing software to cope with the change in date, and developing sophisticated contingency plans that involved hiring power generators, central banks providing increased liquidity in the markets, and governments having emergency services on standby.

4 *Monitor and control.* Risks are rarely static and because they are associated with future events, there will come a time when they will either materialize or no longer pose a threat. This requires the organization to continue to monitor risks once raised in order to assess any changes in impact or probability. In addition, this stage involves allocating responsibility for their management, which includes tracking actions to mitigate them and reporting on their status.

Risk management – banking – The approach to risk management within the banking community differs quite considerably from the process described above. Risk management in banking usually involves:

» setting global target earnings and risk limits;
» translating the goals into business unit target revenues, risk limits, and guidelines; and
» establishing processes for the monitoring and reporting of risks at the transaction as well as the consolidated level. The aggregated figures are used to manage the bank's overall risk.

Risk rating agencies – The two most widely accepted credit risk-rating agencies are Moody's and Standard & Poor's. Both are considered to have the necessary expertise in credit rating and are believed to be unbiased evaluators of an organization's ability to meet its financial obligations. The rating process involves assessing:

» qualitative factors such as the capability of management, the vulnerability of the organization to external change and threats such as regulation, technology, and competition, as well as its growth potential and industrial relations track record; and

» quantitative factors as contained within an organization's financial accounts.

The rating process culminates in the issuing of a credit rating (see separate entry) which determines the terms under which the organization can issue debt. Ratings are usually reviewed once a year taking into account new financial reports and other factors. Because things can change very rapidly with the financial position of an organization, corporations can be subject to a credit watch notice that indicates the rating is likely to change. In most cases this results in a reduction in the credit rating.

Scenario planning – A scenario is a tool for describing, assessing, and understanding possible futures. The process of scenario planning originated in the oil company, Shell, and was used to navigate it through the oil crisis of the 1970s. Scenario planning is an important tool for managing strategic risk, as it allows organizations to think outside the box and consider their future more thoroughly. The process of developing and assessing scenarios usually follows the steps below.

» The existing mental models associated with the organization are captured and challenged as a way of preparing the organization's leaders to revisit their assumptions and open their minds.

» The business context is assessed by taking into consideration political, social, technological, and environmental drivers. These are prioritized according to their importance to the organization.

» The drivers are then used to construct three or four scenarios (essentially narratives describing the future) which are used by the organization to assess their implications and develop strategies that work irrespective of which scenario unfolds.

» The final step is the identification of the leading indicators of each scenario. These will be tracked by the organization as a means of assessing which scenario, or combination of scenarios, is actually unfolding. The indicators are also used to trigger specific actions as defined in the strategy.

The real advantage of scenario planning is that it allows organizations to adapt more quickly to what is happening around them and to anticipate their future more effectively.

Sensitivity analysis – Analysis of the change in the output values of an equation by small changes to the input values, it is used to assess the risk in an investment project.

Settlement risk – The risk that a transaction fails at the time of settlement.

Share capital – Stated in the balance sheet at its nominal value and (if fully paid, and not subject to any share premium) representing the amount of money introduced into the company by its shareholders at the time the shares were issued.

Shareholders' funds – A measure of the shareholders' total interest in the company, represented by the total of share capital plus reserves.

Share premium – The surplus over and above nominal value received in consideration for the issue of shares.

Swaps – Interest rate swaps have been a popular tool for managing risks since the 1980s. They exist because of the differences in interest rates, currency values, and credit ratings of the institutions involved with executing the swap. If, for example, company A has a good credit rating in market X but a poor one in market Y, and company B has a good rating in market Y but a poor one in market X, there is an opportunity to execute a swap. In this instance, company A would borrow money on behalf of company B to allow them to operate in market Y, and *vice versa*. This allows both companies to operate with a reduced risk in their secondary markets.

There are two forms of swaps.

» Interest rate swaps are where the two parties agree to pay the other's interest rate payments when they become due. The swap does not apply to the loan itself, only the interest.

» Currency swaps involve raising a loan in one currency and then swapping it into another at an agreed exchange rate. Debt is serviced in the same way as an interest rate swap, and once the maturity date has been reached, the loan amount will be re-exchanged at a pre-agreed rate.

Technology risk – According to Lewis Branscomb and Philip Auerwald, authors of *Taking Technical Risks*, risk falls into three categories.

» Technical risk. This is associated with the problems that can occur during the development and application of any new or emerging technology. Issues such as safety, security, reliability, and applicability are all relevant.

» The availability of competencies and complementary technologies required to support the introduction of a new technology. This is typically associated with the skills required to implement the new technology, and is most commonly found within IT projects. There are three main risks to manage under this category.

> » Ignorance of prevailing knowledge. Technicians may not be aware of the full extent of the new technology or the techniques used to implement it, even though the organization expects them to understand all aspects of it. With faster cycle times and shortening project horizons, there is often no time to gain the necessary understanding prior to attempting its implementation; the project becomes the training ground, and very often a disaster.

> » Failure to use prevailing knowledge. Although aware of current tools, techniques, and technologies, organizational pressure for rapid implementation often means there is no opportunity to use them. Such time pressure means there is little time to train staff, which in turn reduces the chances of implementing the new technology successfully. This has a subsequent knock-on effect in achieving the benefits from the investment.

> » Conditions beyond prevailing knowledge. This is the classic leading edge project that involves pioneering activity and trailblazing by the experts, using hitherto untried and untested technologies, tools, or techniques.

» Specification achievability. This is associated with the outcome of the technology implementation in terms of its ability to meet the original specification. All too often the requirements, both in terms of functionality and performance, are not met. Once again this will affect the business case, the benefits, and the long-term value of the product if it is to be sold on the open market.

Turnover – Revenue from sales.

Value at Risk (VaR)[4] – Value at Risk is defined as the worst loss that might be expected from holding a security or portfolio over a given period of time and given a specified level of probability. The strict definition is "the maximum loss over a given period such that there is a 1% probability that the actual loss over the given period will be larger." VaR does not state the full extent of the loss, it merely indicates how likely it is that the loss will exceed the VaR figure.

Calculating the VaR involves:

» deriving the forward distribution of the portfolio (or the return on the portfolio at a given point in the future). This distribution is either assumed to follow a normal distribution (parametric VaR) or from historical data (non-parametric VaR); and

» calculating the first percentile of the forward distribution.

VaR is the maximum loss at the 99% confidence level relative to the expected value of the portfolio at the target horizon.

VaR not only provides a consistent approach to managing risks across an institution, but also ensures risks are visible rather than hidden from view. In addition, it doubles up as a senior management reporting tool and is an important consideration when deriving credit ratings.

Variable cost – A cost that increases or decreases in line with changes in the level of activity.

Volatility – One of the basic statistical measures of risk. The volatility of an investment portfolio is directly related to how far its value varies from the mean. There are two methods for measuring the volatility in financial markets. The first is to use historical data about the investment. Although useful as a way of establishing trends, it can never be fully relied upon because the level of volatility will depend upon the period over which the data is gathered. The second is to use models such as Black-Scholes to estimate the volatility.

Working capital - Current assets less current liabilities, representing the amount a business needs to invest and which is continually circulating in order to finance its stock, debtors, and work in progress.

Work in progress - Goods (or services) in the course of production (or provision) at the balance sheet date.

NOTES

1 Barnes, J.C. (2001) *A Guide to Business Continuity Planning*. John Wiley & Sons, Chichester, p. 19.

2. For more detail see *Fraud Prevention Guide*, ClearCommerce white paper.

3 Holiwell, J. (1998) "Risk: Enough rope to hang the business?" In: *Mastering Finance: The Definitive Guide To The Foundations And Frontiers Of Finance*. Financial Times Pitman Publishing, London, pp. 293-7.

4 Crouhy M., Galai, D. & Mark, D. (2001) *Risk Management*. McGraw-Hill, New York, pp. 187-92.

Resources

Plenty has been written about risk management, and it covers a great raft of material. Chapter 9 identifies some of the many resources available:

» books
» websites
» magazines.

"Since the 1970s, more than US$100bn in operational losses have occurred as a result of processing failures, fraud and system disruption. In the last 30 years, there have been over 2000 events with an average 'per event' loss of US$70mn."

Algorithmics risk management consultancy

"If you are sure you understand everything that is going on, you are hopelessly confused."

Walter Mondale, US Senator

Risk is a well-researched topic, with plenty of books, courses, magazines, articles, and tools to keep the risk manager up to date with the latest thinking and standard concepts of risk management. The following resources are designed to provide a general review of the subject of risk in its widest sense, from financial risk management through to operational, technical, and project risk.

BOOKS

The following books cover the key topics within risk and risk management.

Roger Lowenstein (2001) *When Genius Failed: The Rise and Fall of Long-Term Capital Management.* Fourth Estate, London

This is required reading for anyone who wants to understand the risks associated with hedging. Long-Term Capital Management was significant in that it almost brought down the world's financial system. Created by Nobel Award winners and well-known investment bankers, the fund racked up returns of over 40% per annum on its $100bn in assets, virtually all of which was borrowed from the major global investment banks. The problem with the fund was that it had entered into thousands of derivative contracts with a combined exposure of over $1trn. And when the Russians defaulted on their loans, the fund suffered major losses day after day and as a result was on the verge of defaulting itself. It was only through the intervention of the global investment banks, which had invested in the fund in the first place, that the world's financial system was saved from almost certain disaster.

Michael Crouhy, Dan Galai & Robert Mark (2001) *Risk Management*. McGraw-Hill, New York

A comprehensive guide on risk management in banking, with chapters on the regulatory environment, credit rating systems, Value at Risk, operational risk, capital allocation and performance measurement and risk management in nonfinancial institutions.

Peter Bernstein (1996) *Against the Gods: The Remarkable Story of Risk*. John Wiley & Sons, New York

Probably the best historical analysis of financial risk management available. This book traces the development of numbering systems, the emergence of probability, as well as the development of the practice of risk management. As well as the historical angle, the resource discusses risk management techniques and processes, such as options and derivatives, outlines the problems and issues associated with managing risk and details the implications of computers. An important read for anyone interested in understanding why risk management is a crucial skill in today's complex world.

Jean Camp (2001) *Trust and Risk in Internet Commerce*. The MIT Press, Cambridge, MA

This book discusses in detail the nature of risk within e-commerce. The beauty of this resource is that it covers some of the basics before dealing with the specific risks of e-commerce and how organizations can respond to them (see also Chapter 4 and Chapter 6 for more on the risks of online merchandising). The early chapters cover the evolution of the Internet and how it works, the nature of money, and cryptography. It then moves onto aspects of security and the tools that are used to make online transactions secure (such as the public key system and digital certificates and signatures). Because online commerce involves the merchant and purchaser trusting each other, Camp spends some time discussing the nature of privacy both in terms of the law and in practice. He follows this by examining the nature of Internet transactions, e-commerce systems and rounds the book off by discussing various Internet currencies.

Joël Bessis (1998) *Risk Management in Banking*. John Wiley & Sons, Chichester

A resource that offers a comprehensive coverage of all aspects of risk management within banking, split into 11 parts. Each part covers in minute detail elements of risk management, ranging from the nature of risk in financial services, through to hedging, portfolio management, and transfer pricing. In essence, if you want to know anything about managing risks in banking, this is the book to read.

Peter Schwartz and Blair Gibb (1999) *When Good Companies Do Bad Things*. John Wiley & Sons, New York

This is a particularly useful reference for those organizations who have a presence in developing countries, or whose operations have environmental consequences. It tackles the issues that have arisen from globalization, especially in relation to the need for increased social and corporate responsibility. They trace the history of public opinion and big business by looking at the slave trade, the rise of the railroads, and the rise of the imperial corporation and follow this by a detailed look at modern-day corporations including Shell, Unocal, Nestlé, Union Carbide, Texaco, and Nike. Having introduced the issues, the main thrust of the book is to provide the basis for managing the risks of globalization by improving social and corporate responsibility. Plenty of advice is given on what constitutes best practice in this increasingly important area.

Lewis Branscomb and Philip Auerswald (2001) *Taking Technical Risks*. The MIT Press, Cambridge, MA

This book is based upon a joint Harvard-MIT project on managing technical risk. It focuses on the two major issues that face any technical innovation: product failure and market failure. In doing so, it outlines the product development processes, how risks and rewards are defined, and how corporations can leverage their investments in new technology. The key chapter within the book is Chapter IV, which specifically looks at the strategies for managing product and market risk. The book also casts its net more widely by looking at government policy, funding issues, and the role of universities.

William Boni and Gerald Kovacich (1999) *I-Way Robbery*. Butterworth-Heinemann, Boston

This book traces the rise of Internet crime. Starting with a review of Internet technologies and how they can benefit the organization, it then moves on to the specific problem of Internet crime. The early chapters trace the history of crime and how the ability to commit crime has advanced in step with technological change. As expected in a book such as this, the legal and policy aspects of Internet crime are discussed in some detail. Chapter 5 is especially useful for the risk manager because it describes the motivations behind the people who carry out Internet crime. The authors believe that understanding the motivations of the Internet criminal is a sound way to begin to manage the risks they pose. Having identified the motivations, the next couple of chapters identify the targets they are interested in (business information and so on), together with how the crimes are actually executed. Only then do the authors focus on the basic security measures that can be taken to counter the threats and manage the risks. This book augments Jean Camp's book discussed above.

Chris Frost, David Allen, James Porter, and Philip Bloodworth (2001) *Operational Risk and Resilience*. Butterworth-Heinemann, Oxford

This book aims to provide the risk manager with an up-to-date perspective on the importance of operational risk and its management. In particular, the authors position risk management as a means of improving shareholder value, rather than just a defensive mechanism for preventing financial loss. The arguments for a renewed look at operational risk stem from the increasing complexity of business activities. The book begins with an overview of risk management and covers sources of operational risk and the importance of control frameworks. The majority of the book concentrates on two key elements: operational integrity and operational delivery. Both sections provide ample examples and details on how to assess and manage operational risk. The book rounds off with a look at twenty-first century operational risk that understandably focuses on the increased complexity of risk factors (including the implications of globalization, the increasing dependence on information systems, and rapid change).

Kees van der Heijden (1996) *Scenarios, The Art of Strategic Conversation*. John Wiley & Sons, Chichester

This book has been included because of the importance of scenario planning in the management of strategic and business risk. The book uses Shell as a case study throughout, which provides an excellent example of how scenario planning can benefit the organization (see Chapter 7, which discusses how Shell has used and benefited from scenario planning). The book begins by discussing why planning is an important discipline within organizations. It follows this by detailing the three paradigms of strategic management (rationalistic, evolutionary, and processual) and how these can be integrated through the concept of institutional learning. The bulk of the book focuses on the process of scenario planning and how this benefits the organization.

Chris Chapman and Stephen Ward (1997) *Project Risk Management*. John Wiley & Sons, Chichester

There are very few books that deal exclusively with project risk management. The book offers a general approach to the management of project risk that is based upon the authors' eight-stage project life cycle (conceive, design, plan, allocate, execute, deliver, review, and support). The authors' risk management process has nine phases (define, focus, identify, structure, ownership, estimate, evaluate, plan, and manage). Having defined the process and discussed each stage in detail (which is done in a practical and applied way), the authors concentrate on how the risk management process can be applied to specific examples. The process offered is sufficiently generic to be used in all types of projects and programs.

WEBSITES

ClearCommerce® (www.clearcommerce.com)

ClearCommerce® supplies businesses with secure, fully integrated automated payment processing software for the Internet. Its products are suitable for online, secure real time payment, as well as more traditional forms of payment through call centers. With fraud rates for Internet transactions 10 times that of bricks and mortar companies, the FraudShield product allows merchants to implement an automated screening process tailored to their business. It consists of six layers:

» integration with external security services (such as those used by credit card companies);
» automatic lockouts;
» negative and positive lists (the former being used to lock out credit cards which are being used fraudulently and the latter to develop rules for trusted customers);
» merchant rules that allow the user to create their own fraud rules;
» fraud analyzer, which is a neural network model that brings the merchant collective risk assessment intelligence gathered from other merchants and e-commerce transactions; and
» case management tool that provides automated alerts to the merchant's risk management staff to allow them to accept or reject a transaction.

FinancialCAD (www.fincad.com)

FinancialCAD provides an integrated set of financial instrument management software products, financial information, application services, and development tools to those who work with financial instruments. As well as being available on the desktop, these tools are available over the Internet. The Fincad XL product provides access to a library of over 500 industry standard financial modeling functions including interest rate curves, Value at Risk, swaps, and so on. In addition to the functions, Fincad XL includes prebuilt Excel workbook solutions for immediate use. The Internet access allows up-to-date market data to be cut and pasted into Excel workbooks to assess risks in near real time.

Risk Services and Technology (www.risktrak.com)

Risk Services and Technology is a high technology company that is focused on risk management within technology projects. Its services cover software development, information technology, construction, medical device construction, US Department of Defense program management, and earned value management. It also provides other professional services, including independent verification and validation, and technology assessment and development. A software tool, RiskTrak version 5.0, is available for evaluation via their Website.

Algorithmics (www.algorithmics.com)

Algorithmics was founded in 1989 in response to the increasing complexity of financial risk management. The company provides an entire risk management solution offered in a collection of bundled packages that can integrate market, liquidity, credit, and asset liability management under one methodology with one risk architecture (covering market, credit, energy, operational, asset liability management, and limits). The bundled packages share common scenario generation, valuation and risk engines, data transformation components, Web-based and historical reporting tools, and extensibility tools. In addition, Algorithmics takes an active part in advancing the practices of financial risk management through:

» the Algo Quarterly Review;
» risklab.com, which is an international network of risk management research and education establishments that conducts advanced research into financial mathematics and risk management; and
» publications.

Riskworld (www.riskworld.com)

Riskworld is essentially a risk management site that covers all aspects of risk management, from financial through to environmental. It is a one-stop shop for everything associated with risk and risk management. It includes the following.

» A bookstore that contains a vast array of books dedicated to the subject of risk management. Major topic headings include financial and investment risks, environmental and ecological risks, health risks, risk assessment and management, and technology risks (including software and biotechnology).
» Publications that cover risk management journals, abstracts, links to databases that provide information on a variety of risk management

topics (ranging from health risks through to technology), news services, newsletters and magazines, papers and reports.

» News on risk. This provides current risk-related headlines, calls for papers and events. In addition it has a news archive that extends as far back as 1995, together with a press release archive.

» Organizations. This covers associations and societies, centers and institutes, and risk management consultancies.

» Software. Provides links to a large number of software tools arranged in an A–Z format. These tools cover every conceivable form of risk management activity.

This Website is a very useful first point of call for anyone seeking risk management information.

RMRI (www.rmri.com)

RMRI is an international organization providing research and development and consultancy services in asset and risk management. Their risk-based decision management methodology employs a wider definition of risk, that recognizes that a risk is taken when capital of any description is staked under conditions of uncertainty. It allows complex problems to be analyzed in terms of the capital demands of the problem, the returns expected by the stakeholders of the capital, and the uncertainty of the returns themselves. The methodology is designed to provide a consistent approach to managing risk. In addition to the method, RMRI have a number of tools for managing risk, provide training and technology transfer to risk professionals, and have a number papers that can be downloaded, plus a glossary of common risk terms.

RISK MANAGEMENT TOOLS

The following tools are a small selection of the many available to the risk management professional. The tools highlighted below have been selected to cover the areas discussed in this resource.

Winsight (www.cs-solutions.com)

Winsight is an earned value management tool designed to engage technical, schedule, and financial professionals in the management of major projects and programs. The tool is specifically geared to improving project performance, streamlining the process of project management and enhancing the communication with the project's stakeholders.

Crystal Ball® 2000 (www.decisioneering.com)

Crystal Ball® 2000 is a suite of risk analysis tools using the Monte Carlo simulation as its base. The tool can be used with Microsoft® Excel and, depending on the edition used, can provide global optimization and time series forecasting.

Ki4 (www.entegracorp.com)

Ki4 is a reputation risk system aimed at professionals, managers, and executives who are concerned with the management of their business's reputation. The product is essentially an early warning system that allows organizations to organize data associated with corporate incidents and issues. It provides the basis for identifying and tracking problems and trends so that organizations can improve their prevention measures. The basic Ki4 product can be enhanced to allow more active investigating, managing, tracking, and reporting of actual and suspected incidents throughout the organization.

Quest™ (www.envisiontools.com)

Envision Sustainability Tools Inc. focuses on developing computer-based learning tools that allow non-expert users to better understand and respond to sustainability issues they face. Envision has developed tools to suit the needs of regions worldwide and thus can help corporations assess issues of sustainability when siting operations overseas. Their principal product, Quest, allows the specific environmental, economic, and social factors to be modeled in order to create and evaluate alternative scenarios for a given region.

Sierra (www.fnx.com)

FNX Sierra is a financial markets solutions company that provides front, middle, and back office solutions for the international financial community. The Sierra risk management product provides real time global limits against user-defined criteria. Limits against notional amount, risk tolerances, Greeks, profit and loss, future volatility values, collateralized trading, settlement and loss limits are fully supported in real time. FNX has close links with Algorithmics (see above).

Ris³ (www.ris3.com)

Ris³ is a general risk management reporting tool for project management, health and safety management, performance measurement, regulation conformance, and corporate governance. The tool incorporates a number of features, including the following.

» *Risk classification tree*. This is designed to establish a common baseline for risk assessment (see Chapter 8 for a general approach to this) and the cost of implementing risk reduction actions.
» *Risk assessment sheet*. For each identified risk, all relevant data for each phase of the risk management process is displayed on a single page.
» *Risk reporting*. Ris³ can generate a large number of reports including ranking, top risks, trend analyses, action updates, and so on.
» *Quantitative analysis*. The Monte Carlo simulation technique is used to assess the benefit of the risk mitigation against the cost of the risk reduction.

Panorama™ and Opus® (www.risk.sungard.com)

SunGard Trading and Risk Systems has a portfolio of products focused on risk management. The two highlighted here are aimed at market, credit, and operational risks plus advanced interest rate derivative trading and risk management solutions. Panorama™ can be fully integrated within institutions to capture cross-asset trading activity across the firm, aggregate it, and deliver sophisticated market, credit risk management tools to those that need them (remotely, as well as centrally). It supports interest rate products, fixed income, foreign exchange and money markets, equities and equity derivatives, mortgage backed securities, banking instruments, and exotic derivatives. Its risk reporting facilities include Value at Risk, Monte Carlo, scenario analysis, cashflow analysis, and portfolio analysis. Opus® is a cross-product front-to-back-office trading risk management system, comprising cash and derivative instruments in interest rates, equity, credit derivatives, and so on. It provides market feeds, best of breed analytics, exotics, treasury, risk management, and hedging tools.

MAGAZINES

Treasury and Risk Management (www.magazinecity.net)

This is a free magazine that provides the latest trends, news, analysis, and product reviews for chief financial officers, treasurers, directors/vice presidents of finance, and other senior financial executives at US corporations with over $50mn in sales.

Risk Management Magazine (www.rmmag.com)

Risk Management Magazine is a major source of analysis, insight, and news for corporate risk managers. The magazine explores existing and emerging techniques and concepts around the protection of an organization's human, physical, intellectual, and financial assets.

Risk and Insurance (www.riskandinsurance.com)

Risk and Insurance magazine is aimed at key decision makers in the fields of risk management and insurance. The magazine has articles covering the latest trends and events in risk management, insurance, re-insurance, alternative risk transfer, self-insurance, and benefits. The magazine is published monthly.

CFO (www.cfo.com)

CFO is written and edited specifically for senior executives with financial responsibility. Published monthly in the US, Europe, and Asia, *CFO* provides in-depth strategic information covering topics that range from core financial practices to the impacts of e-business.

Collections and Credit Risk (www.ccr.faulknergray.com)

An online magazine focusing on the management of credit risk. It provides latest views of the industry, portfolio management, credit risk technology, economic outlook, and reviews/case studies of organizations involved in the management of credit risk management.

Credit Card Management (www.ccm.faulknergray.com)

Another online magazine, this time geared to the issues and trends in credit card management. It provides an industry watch on card issues, discusses topics such as credit card debt and online fraud, and has special reports on hot topics, such as telemarketing, e-payments, and so on.

Ten Steps to Making Risk Management Work

Being successful at risk management means:

» understanding your risk appetite;
» formalizing the process;
» identifying and categorizing risk at all levels;
» managing risks actively;
» developing a risk culture;
» learning from the successes and mistakes of others;
» asking yourself difficult questions;
» using known methods and tools;
» using expert advice; and
» remembering to balance risk and reward.

"Trying to be explicitly logical about alternative decisions, uncertain events, probability beliefs and preferences can clarify your objectives and your understanding of the risks and opportunities that you face. In many cases, the process of applying these risk management techniques can suggest much better decisions than those that would have otherwise occurred to you."

Dan Borge, managing director and partner, Bankers Trust
"What would life be if we had no courage to attempt anything?"
Vincent van Gogh, artist

Risk management is both an art and a science, and being successful depends on how well the two are kept in balance. The following 10 steps to success will provide those concerned with the management of risk with the basis on which to establish and maintain this balance.

1. UNDERSTAND YOUR RISK APPETITE

Understanding what risks the organization is willing to take helps to define the boundary between acceptable and unacceptable risks. The level of risk-taking should feed into the strategic intent of the organization and, more importantly, frame how the organization intends to manage them. Chris Frost, David Allen, James Porter, and Philip Bloodworth, authors of *Operational Risk and Resilience*, believe organizations should ask themselves the following five questions in order to understand their risk appetite.

» What risks is the organization prepared to take in pursuit of its business goals and where is the boundary between these and those risks it is unwilling to take?
» Are the risks consistent with the organization's strategy?
» Where should exposure to risk be reduced?
» Is the organization too risk adverse and as a result missing opportunities?
» How will the organization's stakeholders be affected by the risks being taken?

In answering these questions, the organization will know those risks it is willing to take, understand that some risks are necessary if it is to succeed in its allotted market, know how it intends to manage the risks it wishes to take, and avoid those it doesn't. These questions should also be applied to the individual functions, as this will ensure that the risks are known throughout the whole organization and, more importantly, help to create a healthy risk management culture.

2. FORMALIZE THE PROCESS

Relying on instinct, gut feel, or raw judgment is never the best way to manage risk. The inherent danger of relying on this type of approach is that things will be missed, information will not be captured or shared, and risks will be either badly managed, or not managed at all. This makes risk management a lottery and can lead to very nasty surprises. And we have all seen how extreme the consequences of poor risk management can be from the financial disaster at Barings Bank, the bursting of the dotcom bubble, and the oil crisis of 1973.

Formalizing the process of risk management ensures that everyone is aware of the dangers that lurk within their business and what is to be done about them. The process should be documented and actively managed, by the appointment of risk officers throughout the enterprise, and by ensuring that the identification, management, and reporting of risk is part of everyone's objectives. Formalizing the process also ensures that the organization is able to prioritize its risk management actions by focusing on those risks that have the largest impact and highest probability. It also means that the balance between the cost of managing a risk and its associated financial impact on the firm if it materializes is appropriately balanced.

3. IDENTIFY AND CATEGORIZE RISKS AT ALL LEVELS

Risk occurs at all levels in the organization; strategically, within major projects and programs, and operationally. Increasingly the source and nature of risk is becoming more diverse. Factors such as globalization, the Internet, and rapid technological change have all served to introduce new risks that have to be managed. Formalizing the process, as per step 2, above, ensures that risks are identified. But in order to manage them effectively, it is essential that they are appropriately categorized so that they are dealt with at the correct level within the organization and that suitably qualified personnel are involved with their management. The typical risk categories that organizations should concern themselves with are as follows:

» credit risk
» country and transfer risk
» interest rate risk
» strategic and business risk
» program and project risk
» liquidity risk
» foreign exchange risk
» reputation risk
» market risk
» operational risk
» product/technical risk
» financial risks arising from internal and external fraud
» legal risk
» regulatory risk.

4. MANAGE RISKS ACTIVELY

Many organizations believe, quite wrongly, that the process of risk management stops at capturing and categorizing the risks. Such organizations also believe that risk management is a passive, not an active, process. The biggest problem in adopting the passive stance is that it leads to surprises and forces the organization to fire fight and crisis manage. Such fire fighting is a chronic waste of organizational resource and can do untold damage to a corporation's reputation. Active risk management, however, involves continuously scanning the internal and external horizons for potential risks, taking time to understand what they might mean for the organization, and taking positive decisions as to whether they will be managed or not. Although perhaps less exciting than fire fighting, such an approach not only allows organizations to manage risk more effectively, it also allows them to spot opportunities more readily. And it is the ability to spot opportunities and manage the risks associated with them that differentiates the market leaders from their competitors.

5. DEVELOP A RISK CULTURE

Creating a culture that accepts and embraces risk is essential to being effective at risk management. The increasing complexity of the business environment necessitates a more mature approach to managing risk. Organizations can no longer afford to maintain a culture that blames, ignores, or sanitizes failure, as this prevents risks from being spotted in the first place, let alone managed and reported on. Creating a no-surprise culture means allowing everyone to raise concerns and issues as they go about their daily work. Sanctioning those that highlight risks or those that fail only helps to push risk management off the agenda and promote a culture of self-preservation. In the long run this stifles innovation and results in a culture where no one is willing to take risks.

The culture of risk management must, of course, begin with the board of directors, as if it fails here, it will fail throughout the entire organization. Therefore, the creation of a chief risk officer at board level is a positive action that clearly demonstrates the commitment to the management of risk. Similar roles need to be established across each of the major functions to ensure full coverage and commitment. Such roles must be augmented by committees that are geared to the active management of particular risk categories. These usually include some or all of the following:

» business risk management committees;
» operational risk management committees;
» credit risk management committees; and
» program and project boards.

Ultimately, the creation of a healthy risk management culture is designed to reduce the likelihood of shock events and minimize the incidence of irrational behavior within key members of staff, be they on the board, working in the front office, or in control of safety critical processes and systems. Organizations that can create a culture that embraces risk and recognizes the importance of coming clean when mistakes are made (see below) will be more successful than those that don't.

6. LEARN FROM MISTAKES (YOURS AND OTHER PEOPLE'S)

When things go wrong, the way organizations respond depends on their underlying culture and whether there is a high level of fear associated with failure. Where the fear of failure is high and the culture hard – that is, brutish and unforgiving – there is a tendency to blame and sack staff rather than learn from the failure. In such instances, the blame and associated removal of staff is normally misdirected and is rarely the result of a full and thorough analysis of what went wrong, and where the true accountability lay. The problem with this type of reaction is that it creates a culture in which the fear of failure is reinforced. It also forces risks underground and tends to increase the likelihood of the organization repeating its past mistakes.

In organizations where the fear of failure is equally high, but the culture more forgiving, there is a bias toward brushing failures under the carpet and trying to forget that they had ever happened. Once again this limits the ability to manage risk properly. It is where the fear of failure is low that the ability to learn from past experiences is maximized, although not always carried through. For example, where the fear of failure is low and culture unforgiving, the usual response to failure is a "going through the motions" post-failure analysis in which the reasons for the failure are analyzed, reviewed, sanitized, and stored without ever reaching those people that could truly benefit. It is as though there is a need to wring the organization's hands as a means of exorcising the failure. Learning is therefore restricted to a limited number of people, and the experience adds no intrinsic value to the future risk management of the organization.

Finally, where the culture is more forgiving and the fear of failure low, the organization is able to genuinely learn from the experience of failure and feed this into the management of future risks. It is this that helps to establish a proper risk management culture.

7. ASK YOURSELF DIFFICULT QUESTIONS

At regular intervals it is a good idea for organizations to ask themselves "what could happen in the future that would put the business at risk?" In asking this question it is essential to focus it on all aspects of the risk continuum, from the strategic level through to the operational. Asking this question offers two distinct advantages. First, it ensures that risk is kept at the forefront of the board's and every functional head's mind. And second, it ensures that the risks that the organization faces are kept current.

8. USE KNOWN METHODS AND TOOLS TO SUPPORT YOU

Effective risk management relies on the discipline of capturing information, tracking the management of risks once identified, and regularly reporting on their status (i.e. their impact, probability, and actions associated with their management). Rather than reinventing the wheel, it is far better to use tried and tested methods and tools to support you. And because there are so many vendors selling risk management tools, methods, and services, there is normally a tool to manage the kinds of risks the organization faces, be they financial, operational, technical, or more general in nature (see Chapter 9 for a small sample).

9. USE EXPERT ADVICE WHERE REQUIRED

Managing risk is not an easy task and sometimes it is necessary to seek professional help. Risk management professionals and specialists can provide advice on both the general aspects of risk management, including process, risk factors, and mitigation strategies, as well as detailed knowledge and advice on specific categories of risk. Although the use of internal auditors is good for assessing controls and generic risks, they often lack the specialist skills of the external expert. They also lack the creativity required to manage risk, as well as the ability to see the upside of risk ... opportunity. Seeking professional help not only improves the risk management process, but it also allows the organization to begin to develop a wider capability in risk management through the effective transfer of knowledge.

10. REMEMBER TO BALANCE RISK WITH REWARD

Managing risk is not all about looking for problems. Ultimately it is about maintaining the balance between risk and reward. The ability to make profits depends on making appropriate decisions, having first assessed the level of return from the investment and the risks it might present. Where these are out of balance, it will either result in a crash and burn scenario, as we saw with the dotcoms, or a slow growth that allows you to become a target for take-over. Balancing risk and opportunity is key because it allows you to push the boundaries of the organization whilst at the same time not betting the company on unnecessary or rash ventures.

KEY LEARNING POINTS

Ten steps to making risk management work

1 Understand your risk appetite. If you do this you will know where your risk boundaries lie.
2 Formalize the process. A repeatable and consistent process is an essential element to risk management.
3 Identify and categorize risks at all levels.
4 Manage risks actively. Risk management is not a passive process.
5 Develop a risk culture. People should be encouraged to raise risks as this ensures they remain visible.
6 Learn from success and mistakes (yours and other people's) – if you can't learn from your own successes and mistakes, you can't expect to learn from others'.
7 Ask yourself difficult questions. This will ensure that the horizon is continuously scanned for potential risks.
8 Use known methods and tools to support you. There is no point in reinventing the wheel.
9 Use expert advice where required; internal knowledge is often lacking.
10 Remember to balance risk with reward.

Frequently Asked Questions (FAQs)

Q1: What is risk management?

A: See Chapter 2 – What is Risk Management?

Q2: Why should I bother with risk management?

A: See Chapter 2 – sections *The consequences of poor risk management* and *Advantages of risk management*; and Chapter 7 – In Practice: Risk Management Success Stories.

Q3: Who is responsible for risk management?

A: See Chapter 6 – section *Risk roles and responsibilities*

Q4: What types of risk do organizations face and how do they deal with them?

A: See Chapter 2 – section *Categories of risk*; Chapter 6 – The State of the Art; and Chapter 7 – In Practice: Risk Management Success Stories.

Q5: Why has risk management evolved to be so important?

A: See Chapter 3 – The Evolution of Risk Management.

Q6: How do organizations manage their risks?

A: See Chapter 7 – In Practice: Risk Management Success Stories.

Q7: What are the implications of the Internet for risk management?

A: See Chapter 4 – The E-Dimension.

Q8: What are the implications of globalization for risk management?

A: See Chapter 5 – The Global Dimension.

Q9: How do I find out more about the subject?

A: See Chapter 9 – Resources.

Q10: How can I succeed in managing risk?

A: See Chapter 10 – Ten Steps to Making Risk Management Work.

Index

accountability, individual   17–18
active management   112
administrative security   55
advantages   12, 13
advice, expert   115
Amnesty International   47
appetite for risk   7–8, 13, 67, 68, 110–11
Asia   38, 39
assessment   65–6
Auerswald, Philip   49, 91
availability error   18, 19
avoidance   9

banking
    case study   66–8
    fees   32
    Internet   11, 30
    investment   17–18, 19–20
    quantitative measures   9–10, 13
Barings Bank   19–20
Barnes, James   77
behavior   17–20, 57
Bernstein, Peter   16
Bessis, Jöel   9–10
Boni, William   55–6
books   96–100

Borge, Dan   6
BP   12
brand risk   66
Branscomb, Lewis   49, 91
BT   49
bubbles   11, 24, 111
business risk   7, 112
business unit managers   58

Cadbury report   21
case studies
    gas utility   70–72
    a global bank   66–8
    Mattel   66
    Nike   40, 68–9
    Shell   3, 40, 62–3
    Standish Group   69–70
    Xerox   64–6
cash flows   49–50
categories of risk   6–7, 13, 112
categorization of risk   111–12
Caux Round Table (CRT)   48
chargebacks   32
chief executive   57
chief financial officer   57
chief risk officer   57
citizenship   41, 47–8

CityReach International   30
CoBit (International)   21
CoCo (Canada)   21
committees   58
complexity, organizational   16-17
computers, unauthorized access
   32-4, 54-6
concepts   76-93
CONFIRM project   70
conformity error   18
consistency, misplaced   19, 20
control   20-23, 67
corporate citizenship   41, 48
corporate complexity   16-17
corporate governance   20-22
COSO (USA)   20-21
costs   31-2
country risk   41-3, 112
credit card fraud   32
credit risk   10, 112
crisis scenario   62-3
culture, organizational   56, 58, 113
cybercrime   33-4, 46, 54-5

data currency   31
democratic institutions   48
diamond industry   39-40
disclaimers, emails   51-2
distortion of evidence   19
dotcoms   24, 29-30, 43, 49, 111
downside measures   10
downside risks   11, 17, 43
drivers   3, 52
Drummond, Helga   16

e-businesses   52
e-dimension   28-35, 51-6
economic cycl
eco
env
err

escalation   18
evidence   19, 20
evolution   16-24
exchange risk   42
executives, senior   17, 19-20, 57
expert advice   115
exploitation, workforce   17,
   39-40, 46

financial impact   3, 10
financial risk   7, 66-8, 71-72, 112,
   51-6, 41-3
foreign exchange risk   112
formalization of process   111
fraud   31-2, 54, 112, 46
future risk management   58-9

gas utility case study   70-72
Gibb, Blair   39, 46, 48
global bank case study   66-8
global citizenship   47-8
global dimension   38-44
globalization   3, 17, 39-41, 46-9,
   68-9
glossary   76-93
goods sold costs   32
governance, corporate   20-22
group behavior, errors   17, 18-19
Guidance on Control   21
*A Guide to Business Continuity
   Planning*   77

hacking   32-3, 55
halo effect   18
Heijden, Kees van der   63
Hilton, Anthony   43
history   16-24
man rights   48
Hyatt Hotels   70

I-Way Robbery   55
identification stage   8, 111-12

indicators, quantitative 9-10
individual behavior 17-18, 2
interest rate risk 112
internal audit responsibilities 57
international knowledge transfer 39
Internet 2-3, 11, 29-34, 52-4
irrational behaviors 17-20
IT control standards 21

JDS Uniphase 11

key aspects
  concepts 76-93
  frequently asked questions
    117-18
  glossary 76-93
  resources 96-107
  ten steps 110-16
  thinkers 76-93, 96-100
Knight, Phil 68-9
knowledge transfer 39
Kourdi, Jeremy 52
Kovacich, Gerald 55-6

Leeson, Nick 17-18, 19-20
legal risk 112
Levi Strauss 41
liquidity 49, 112
loans 42-3
location risk 42
logistics 67

magazines 106-7
managing stage 9
market risk 10, 64-6, 112
Mattel case study 66
"me-too" risk 29
metrics 9-10, 13, 53
mitigation 56
monitoring stage 9
multiple risks 70-72

neighborhood risk 42
New Economy Edge 52
NGOs (nongovernmental
  organizations) 40, 47, 48-9, 73
Nike case study 40, 68-9

online fraud 31-2, 54, 112, 46
operational risk 7, 56, 70, 72, 112
Operational Risk and Resilience 7
operational security 55
operations management 56
organizational complexity 16-17
organizational culture 56, 58, 113
organizational responsibilities 57-8
over-commitment 17-18, 53

pay disparities 68-9
physical security 55
policies, operational risk 56
political risk 42
primacy error 18, 19
process formalization 111
process stages 8-9, 13, 67, 111
product risk 64-6, 112, 30-31,
  49-51
program managers 57-8
program risk 7, 11, 71, 72, 112
project managers 57-8
project risk 7, 11, 71, 72, 112
public decisions 19

quantification stage 8-10

recessions 43
regulations 20-23
regulatory risk 70, 71, 112
reputation risk 112
resources 96-107
responding stage 9
responsibility 17-18, 41,
  48-9, 57-8
responsible commercial success 41

risk assessment 65-6
risk control 20-23, 67, 9
risk culture development 113
risk management committees 58
risk/reward balance 115-16
robustness of product 30-31
roles 57-8

scenarios 47, 62-3
Scenarios: The Art of Strategic Conversation 63
Schwartz, Peter 6, 38, 39, 46, 48
security, computer access 32-4, 54-6
senior executives 17, 19-20, 57
sensitivity 10
shareholder value 58
Shell case study 3, 40, 62-3
shipping costs 32
shopping, Internet 2-3, 31
social responsibility 41, 48-9
sophistication 7-8
sovereign risk 42
stages, risk management 8-9, 13, 67, 111
stakeholders 47
standards 20-22, 47-8
Standish Group case study 69-70
stereotypes 19
strategic risk 6-7, 56, 62-3, 112

success 41, 69-70
sustainable development 48

Taking Technical Risks 49, 91
technical risk 7, 30-31, 49-51, 64-6, 70, 112
technological change 3
Tesco 2-3, 31
Third Generation telecommunications 49
thinkers 76-93, 96-100
tools 103-6, 115
transfer risk 42, 112
Treadway Commission 20-21
trickle-up product development 50-51
Turnbull standard (UK) 21

unauthorized computer access 32-4, 54-6
utility case study 70-72

value at risk 10
value-based reporting 58
viruses 33
volatility 10

Website design 31
Websites 100-103
workforce exploitation 17, 39-40, 46

Xerox case study 64-6

Printed and bound in the UK by
CPI Antony Rowe, Eastbourne